BEYOND
BETRAYAL

Table Talks

Jerry Price, MA, and Tom Roy

CROSSBOOKS
PUBLISHING

CrossBooks™
A Division of LifeWay
1663 Liberty Drive
Bloomington, IN 47403
www.crossbooks.com
Phone: 1-866-879-0502

For information contact:
Jerry Price
www.jerryprice.net
jp@jerryprice.net
Tom Roy
www.upi.org
troy@upi.org

First published by CrossBooks 10/22/2012

ISBN: 978-1-4627-2229-7 (sc)
ISBN: 978-1-4627-2227-3 (e)
ISBN: 978-1-4627-2228-0 (hc)

Library of Congress Control Number: 2012919513

Printed in the United States of America

CONTENTS

DEDICATION

To all who have been wounded by betrayal,

and to all in the struggle to

embrace life beyond betrayal.

What Others Are Saying

I hate this book! For me *Beyond Betrayal* was a hard read, not because Jerry Price and Tom Roy didn't have something to say, but because what they said is true. Sadly and personally, I can attest to that!

JUDAS ISCARIOT
Betrayer of Jesus

"Authors Jerry Price and Tom Roy lead the reader into a conversation about the inner most world of relationships with others. These relationships, they point out, trace a history of betrayal, pain, hiding, anger, and broken trust lived out before the face of our Creator who loves us. Though written in an easy conversational style, the interactive discussion of the authors is richly layered and nuanced, especially when discussing such topics as betrayal, openness, trust, and forgiveness. The book surfaces the struggle, pain, disappointment, and failure of relationships and points out that the best way forward is to embrace these realities assured that God loves and pursues us. And this God continues reaching out to us, longing to bring help and healing to fallen and broken relationships in which we live. With candor the book calls all readers to embrace our brokenness and experience the mercy and grace of God. A good read about all relationships."

RON MANAHAN, Th.D.
President of Grace College and Seminary Winona Lake, Ind.

When I was a child, we often had guests for dinner. Sometimes they'd stay late into the evening and we children would be put to bed. I remember many nights perching my ear against the wall to hear the adult conversations happening in the next room. I would catch little bits of pain but mostly wisdom and counsel. Reading *Beyond Betrayal* evoked that same curiosity I held as a child, to hear the wisdom of my elders, to be let in on the secrets of life. And, here in this book the doors are wide open and the voices of Tom Roy and Jerry Price speak clearly enough for a child to hear. This is a beautiful working out of life between two wise souls and they let us in on the conversation. They offer a real look at the twisted thinking behind betrayal, the pain and ramifications that come through the acts of betrayal, but mostly the hope that we have to heal from the wounds of betrayal. It is a conversation that ultimately encourages life. That is a conversation I want to have over and over again.

JANA HOLLAND
The Hollands! www.thehollands.org

Beyond Betrayal is a book for those who are serious about understanding our sin nature and its manifestation in the act of betrayal. Those of us who have been betrayed and who are also betrayers can gain sometimes painful insight into this monster – betrayal. Jerry and Tom's book has given me an understanding of the betrayal I faced in my work several years ago. Thank the Lord that bitterness did not set in; otherwise, I may not have withstood the unexpected assault. God defines who we are…not the betrayers who seemingly are bent on our personal destruction. Very deep thanks to Jerry and Tom for their work.

MIKE VALENTINE,

Believer, Husband, Father, Grandfather, Trial Lawyer, *betrayer*

I have known Tom Roy for over 20 years as his friend and as his pastor. I can say without question that there are few people I know that have the experience and perspective Tom does on human nature. Jerry and Tom together have written a wonderful book on one of the most common, overlooked and damaging topics in life. Betrayal has left its mark on all of us and drives our behavior more than we will ever know. Looking at the subject comprehensively gives us an understanding of what has been done to us and what we do to others so we can break the cycle and begin the healing process. I highly recommend this book for anyone who is or has ever been caught in the cycle of betrayal.

DENNY WILSON,

Senior Pastor, Warsaw Community Church

Jerry Price and Tom Roy have tackled the tough and potentially uncomfortable subject of betrayal head on. Previously, I had underestimated the importance of just how significant this can be, but their insight and illustrations have given me a better understanding of its scope and presence in my life.

SCOTT SANDERSON

Pro Sports Agent and Former MLB Pitcher

People will align themselves closely to the hearts of those that they will betray, whether intentional or unintentional, which makes the pain of the betrayal that much greater. Unfortunately, it is more common than we want to believe. Its high frequency manifests itself in the workplace under the false pretense of *"It's just business, it's not personal."* As if that were some form of hall pass to enact individual or organizational betrayal against one another. There is healing hope in the principals shared in this book along with pivotal tools in facing the betrayal of others as well as the temptation to betray."

MIKE MORFORD

CEO & Founder of Greatoutdoors.com

I have never thought much about betraying or being betrayed by others. As I started to read *Beyond Betrayal* I found myself asking, what does this have to do with me? By the time I finished reading, I realized it has everything to do with me and how I lived with those around me. Tom and Jerry show us that understanding how we have been betrayed and have betrayed others is only the first step. Getting beyond betrayal is a quick, easy read but has the integrity not to betray its readers by sharing with us that the final steps to a life lived free of betrayal and it's pain is neither quick or easy, but well worth it.

J. DAVIS ILLINGWORTH JR
Author of God of Hope
Former Senior Vice President Chief Planning and Administrative Officer of Toyota Motor Sales,
U.S.A., Inc

Beyond Betrayal presents a new approach to a sensitive subject. You are welcomed into the living room with Jerry Price and Tom Roy as they discuss this all-too-common and always hurtful experience, betrayal. The reader will enjoy and be enlightened by Jerry's straight forward responses to Tom's insightful questions while being challenged to seek application in their own lives.

JOHN J. SULLIVAN
Author of *My Betrayer is at Hand*

I have been betrayed many times throughout my life. We all have. God's grace and mercy have carried me through those betrayals giving me peace and allowing me to forgive my betrayers. The hardest realization from reading this book has been seeing the *Betrayer* in myself...and again...God's grace and mercy swoops in, filling me with the courage to make amends where possible and to be more aware of my actions and motives. I am so very grateful Tom and Jerry had these *Table Talks* and for sharing them - thanks be to God!

SANDRA ROBISON McCARTHY
Divorce Recovery Group Facilitator

FOREWORD

We don't often use the word "betrayal," but as we read Jerry and Tom's work we became aware of many instances of betrayal in our own lives, our own work, and our own ministry.

Gradually we began to realize that we had experienced betrayal on several occasions, from someone we had trusted—a parent, siblings, relatives, neighbors, friends, co-workers, team members, ministry leaders, and even a pastor. One might expect betrayal from a stranger or an enemy, but not from a good friend, a close associate, or a relative.

Betrayal has come to us in the form of broken promises, moral failures, betrayed confidences, failures to follow through or even to show up, being "thrown under the bus," broken contracts, backstabbing, profound confusion, and outright lies. We have felt obsolete, abandoned, assaulted, obliterated, ignored, and erased—all results of betrayal.

Meanwhile, some of it has been accidental, some has been purposeful, and sometimes we might have seen it where it didn't really exist. But all of it has been painful, and most has come like a shot out of the blue. Totally unexpected. An illegal hit. A foul ball or a stolen base.

One definition that has resonated with us is "thwarting another out of something that ought to occur."[1] The act of betrayal violates one's understanding of rules, roles, relationships, respect, morals, ethics, and values.

Reis and Rusbult said that "Forgiveness of betrayal is exhibited by the victim . . . (when he does not demand) atonement and retribution, and is only complete . . . (when) the victim does not . . . demand apologies or review the incident again and again."[2]

In most of our experiences of betrayal we have chosen to forgive the betrayer and have not demanded atonement and retribution. Life is too short and too precious to stay stuck waiting for the perpetrator to make things right.

Our hope is that reading this book will take you beyond betrayal—to comfort, healing, restoration, renewal, re-connections, and re-established relationships. May loyalty, trust, moral and legitimate boundaries make up the new foundation on which you rebuild betrayals into reliable friendships and allegiances.

You can trust the words of the two authors of this book, both of whom are well-seasoned leaders and dear friends of ours. Their insights bring light, hope, and clarity. We urge you to read and apply the wisdom they've included in the pages ahead. That would be a wise choice, and an even wiser one would be to ask for forgiveness "as we forgive those who have trespassed against us."

Norm and Bobbie Evans
The Winning Ways
www.thewinningways.org
Norm was part of the Miami Dolphins Perfect Season Team,
the only undefeated team in NFL history.

INTRODUCTION

Tom Roy and I have been friends for years. Both of us graduated from Grace College in Winona Lake, Indiana. Occasionally, my wife, Judy, and I have hung out with Tom and Carin, at their cabin on Lake Michigan. That's where he asked me to co-write a book on betrayal.

We all have stories to tell, and all of us are developing our own history. But when Tom made his proposal it suddenly dawned on me that most men don't sit around and talk about betrayal in any shape or form. The idea of two men having conversations on the subject grabbed our attention and energized us. So we decided to meet again at Tom's lakeside cabin—and another cabin in Oregon—to create a dialogue about betrayal.

As a former broadcaster, Tom has experience in asking questions and is good at tapping into stuff I wasn't anticipating. But the discussions are genuine and straightforward. There is no pretending to know everything about betrayal, but what we do understand you will find in this book.

Our approach is simple. It's to talk. Having diverse experiences helps to provide some insights, but more than that we want to encourage life *Beyond Betrayal*. Consider this your invitation to go on the journey with us.

Jerry Price
Professional Counselor/Consultant
Bend, Oregon
Author of *Transforming Twisted Thinking*
Founder of *MORE Married Conferences*
www.moremarried.com

BETRAYAL TRAGEDIES

Someone you care about has betrayed you. You never saw it coming. You never imagined anyone this close to you could cause this much hurt. You try to act like everything is fine. Or, you think there must be a better way to handle the pain but you can't figure out what it would be. You may be burying yourself in work or other activities.

Or maybe you are the betrayer. Whether you intended to or not, you betrayed someone close to you. No matter how much you try you can't seem to penetrate the newly erected wall between the two of you. The relationship is broken and you don't know how to fix it.

At some time in our lives, all of us have probably betrayed someone . . . or *been* betrayed. Because someone in your life has hurt you deeply and you are still hurting, maybe you are covering up by being so nice. Or maybe you handle it in a different way. Maybe you are bitchy and live a life filled with continual anger. You want a better way to exist but you find it hard to forgive, or even to figure out who you are. So you count the hours of your loneliness, work more, or become busier in other ways.

Life is not about relationships for you. It may be about winning, making a name, or having a bigger bank account. But what also could be grabbing you is how you, too, might have been a betrayer.

The pages that follow should provide some healing, but they might also cause you more pain. We are not holding back. It is about time for you to live again. Our hope is that you'll be committed to struggling through the following discussions in this book. You—or someone you know—has been hurt so deeply that being called a human being doesn't describe the pain. Being a human time bomb does.

Whatever side of the betrayal dynamic you might be on, these frank and open discussions are intended to stir up the mind and motivate change. But change or healing won't begin until you start talking and deal with the unspeakable.

Welcome to the cabin, and welcome to our straightforward table talks. You are in the room with us and as far as we're concerned, you are part of the discussion.

CHRISTINA'S STORY

My name is Christina. I grew up being physically and verbally abused by my dad, which eventually led to a deep resentment in men and a life that was out of control. He betrayed what love could have meant for me because, as a dad, he's supposed to protect me from the bad things.

Mom didn't protect me from dad either because, in some fear-based way she seemed more concerned about protecting herself and I think betrayed what a mother should stand for too.

I can't blame my siblings for protecting themselves and leaving me there, but it still feels like they betrayed me, as well. Extended family members also knew what was happening, but to my knowledge no one did anything to stop the abuse. It was like a family conspiracy; a dark family secret on both sides.

I believe a direct result from all the secrecy was that, at a very early age, I learned how to betray others. I truly discovered the power of manipulation during my first female encounter at age eighteen and how good at it I was. I'd always heard the strongest craft wasn't what was pulled from a book but what you conjured up from your own desires and passions.

Energy was my passion and manipulating it was my desire. I soon realized that when I projected lots of confidence to other people it was much harder for them to catch on to my manipulation. I got to know their hearts and desires well enough and used what they wanted for my benefit. And yet there were plenty of times when I was left feeling used, unwanted, and lied to by those who couldn't handle or understand me, so it was a real catch 22—like my own pretense came back to me in spades!

Another obvious result from the abuse is that I don't trust people very well and I still put up walls. If I think I'm going to get hurt I will push them away, whether my fear is real or imagined. It takes a lot for someone to be my friend. I'm suspicious, paranoid, and very high maintenance. So, I test others frequently and then push them aside. Or, I leave them hanging.

I've felt betrayed by people—who claimed to be Christians—when they eventually found out about bits and pieces of my abuse. They didn't do much to help and eventually wouldn't let their kids hang around me. Many of the people I've gone to church with also turned their backs on me.

For most of my life I have also felt much betrayed by God. I'd hear about how He loved me and would protect me. To me that didn't make sense, because He gave me to abusive parents and brought people into my life who rejected me.

My escape was the occult. I loved the power I thought I had and felt indestructible at times. I thrived on feeling evil. People were afraid of me but somehow still drawn to me. I tried to be seductive, intriguing, and intimidating.

Eventually, at a point in my life when I was trying to heal, I married my high school sweetheart. When we weren't able to see eye to eye on what marriage looked like and due to past differences, we divorced. I was relieved and devastated at the same time, because now I felt betrayed by love. My whole existence was a mess!

As I look back on my life I've realized I betrayed myself by becoming someone I never wanted to be. But, I didn't realize those early years would have such a profound effect on me—how so many things that happened had damaged me so much.

Now, I'm at the place where I just want to be good with myself, my life, and other people. I want to be able to face things head on and be healed. I don't want to struggle with homosexuality anymore. I don't want to be angry at my parents any longer and I don't want to resent anyone else who held me back or hurt me.

I want to be bold and courageous. I want to be strong and I want to make the right decisions based on God's view and not on how I view the situation, or how I feel about someone. I want to be able to truly come clean about my deeper feelings instead of playing off the same rehearsed feelings I've played with for years.

WHAT REALLY MATTERS

T: Jerry, let's get right into our discussion. I've heard it said that betrayal is something others do to you and bitterness is something you do to yourself. I know we'll address different shades or degrees of that thought in our talks but one thing is for sure, its' clear Christina's story is full of tragedy. And that's where I'd like to start; not only with her story but anyone's story of betrayal. So, after hearing her story, what do you think most people see as the *real* tragedy of betrayal?

J: Tom, I think betrayal tragedies involve asking the question, "Do we think what happened really matters?"

Based on what I've seen and experienced, what really seems to matter is whether we're betrayed by somebody close to us or by a corporation or some other impersonal entity. Yes, there is pain when an organization has betrayed us, but it doesn't pack the same wallop as the loss of relationship we experience when we're betrayed by a spouse, a family member or friend.

That reminds me of a thought in Psalms 55:20-22, when King David talked about the betrayal in his life.

As for this friend of mine, he betrayed me;

He broke his promises. His words are as smooth as cream, but in his heart is war. His words are as soothing as lotion, but underneath are daggers!

Give your burdens to the LORD, and he will take care of you. He will not permit the godly to slip and fall. (NLT)

BEING DISCONNECTED

When someone close betrays us like we saw with Christina's story and with others we'll tell about in this book, it's like that person dies and our grief goes deeper. There's this weird feeling of estrangement to negotiate, because the person is still alive even though the relationship is dead. You may see them in a store, a church, or at family gatherings, and then you'll feel the out-of-body thing because you can't connect yet and you don't want to stay disconnected.

T: Isn't divorce a betrayal of that type then?

J: Yes, a divorce usually introduces many tragic consequences of betrayal. I've seen an offending party realize the error of their ways and try to reconnect with their previous spouse to mend fences, but they can't. They can cry, change dramatically, and truly perform well, but it's as if their betrayal made them a cadaver. And you can't blame the one who was betrayed for viewing the betrayer that way.

I remember going to a funeral parlor with my father, in which all kinds of people stood around the casket. There were flowers everywhere, and music was playing. But no one could connect with the body of the young fellow who had died.

As the mother bent over the casket, I remember my father saying, "*It's not good-bye, it's good night.*" I could see this statement giving her hope for being reconnected in eternity.

But at the time it looked like she and the others were trying to connect with the boy's cadaver, yet nothing was there! We go into a funeral home and it's obvious; the body in a casket is disconnected from those who mourn.

On the other hand, when someone has been through a divorce they could meet their former spouse in a public place and go cold. As I said, it's like being out-of-body; they can't connect anymore. Maybe they want to connect. Maybe they wish they would connect with them again, but it can't be done because there's been a *relational death*. And it's good-bye, not good night. Hope for relationship is gone!

Welcome to the Table Talk: What emotional damage have you seen resulting from divorce? How would you explain the ripple effect on family, friends and other relationships?

LOSING VULNERABILITY AND MISTRUSTING

T: I think another tragedy of betrayal is the loss of vulnerability. Trust has been broken and we are put on guard. It is always worse when we are betrayed by a spouse or a good friend. We feel we can no longer be totally honest or open with the betrayer. There is a wall in the relationship. Sadly, this mistrust often carries over into other relationships.

J: To me, when mistrust becomes the rule, the loss we experience can quickly turn into something much more than just the loss of the relationship itself.

Another profound loss is the fact that something died inside of us, and before we know it we even disconnect from people who haven't betrayed us. We find ourselves locked into a belief in which this proverbial "rule of mistrust" can't be broken—or else!

T: So then, another tragedy is *losing* the ability to trust. Prior to the betrayal we might have been willing to be vulnerable, but now we become more self-protective. When this happens, openness is lost.

Haven't you said it takes longer to build trust after a betrayal because it goes deep into relationships?

J: Yes, but you know what? If we're going to be alive, that means being vulnerable and risking instead of going back into that shell thing. It's a huge dilemma because whatever we do will affect every relationship we have. And that's huge.

In my mind I could think: "If I've been hurt it's understandable for me to pull in a little and create this outer shell by protecting myself like turtles do." But that turtle always remains what it is. A turtle!

On the other hand, we're human, and if we pull in to say, "I am going to protect myself even though I'll lose a sense of freedom and personal vulnerability," then I won't be overly concerned if you don't want me and reject me. And it won't matter if I am free on the inside or not.

Sadly, if I start this hiding thing and watch my back around everyone I used to connect with, I'll become *relationally inauthentic*.

Welcome to the Table Talk: What events, phrases, or words trigger the "shell thing" for you? In your life, how do you prevent being relationally invulnerable to stay authentic?

Becoming the Betrayer

J: So, I think the deep tragedy coming from a friend or loved one's betrayal is how we're *on the edge* of making decisions to be inauthentic with people. I think this is very important to understand.

If we choose to be inauthentic *we become the betrayer* by living a life of duplicity. And that *will* incarcerate our *own* souls.

We'll be in our cage and all we can see is what we see in that cage, which means that people will never get to know who we really are. We'll become liars; we'll live in a world of pretense and we'll develop fantasies that we believe will allow us to be in absolute control. Sadly, when we settle for that I think we dehumanize ourselves and cease to be alive.

It's heartbreaking!

T: The picture that comes to my mind is the Heisman trophy. It's a great award, but the player in the statue is stiff-arming the tackler and protecting the football. He is keeping others at a distance. He looks good *because* he's isolating himself.

In football and other sports, sometimes it's absolutely essential to do that. That's part of the game. But in churches, in business, and in friendships there are many people who live real life in the same way. They have been hurt in the past and don't want to leave themselves open again. Relationships never get below the surface. That's a tragedy. Another scenario of betrayal can happen in an office or a military setting where others are in positions of authority over us and we don't speak up when things aren't quite right. We don't want to risk our jobs, our financial position, or our status. Rather than talk things out we stuff our emotions. We may then become more closed in our personal lives, like the guy who sits with the remote and a beer. We become that relational turtle you talked about and we stop being truly *alive*.

On Empty

J: Do you remember the song lyric, "What the world needs now is love, sweet love?" When Diana Ross sang that song she would come down off the stage and have the people in the audience hold hands. Everyone would happily rock back and forth while repeating those words.

Tom, here's where I'm going with that thought.

If life is about hiding from people and trying to protect ourselves from the possibility of being betrayed, I believe we lose the ability to love and we become relationally empty. We don't want to hold hands with anyone! But we're in a dilemma because people are *built* to love and to *want* to be loved!

So, if I decide—whether consciously or subconsciously—to put myself in a position to make sure I'm never betrayed again, I'll start manipulating people to guarantee that won't happen. It's a vicious, slippery slope to personal ruin and it ultimately results in my failure to love others. I even betray myself by refusing to risk a relationship with me! Talk about the tragedy of betrayal. How empty is that?

Back in the 80s, while attending Grace College in Winona Lake, Indiana, I became their cross country coach. But I was one of those student fill-in coaches who had never coached the sport before. So I decided to start running, and eventually I liked long-distance running so much that I began to train for marathons.

One cool evening, on a training run around the lake, I started passing other runners. I recall seeing a guy about three hundred yards ahead of me. I was feeling pretty good and wanted to see if I could pass him.

So, I kicked it in and the strangest thing happened with my body. They call it the *runner's high.* I felt like I was floating on air! It was like I could run on water and just keep going. And then I passed the guy. I mean, it was like I came out of nowhere, baby!

I remember thinking, "There I am. That's me!" I was in touch with myself in a way I had never been before, and experienced great joy. It took a sprint, but before that it took long-distance running and some pain to get to that moment in time. In feeling this different *me,* I got in touch with the thought that no one else did this but me. And I liked it.

But if I'm betrayed and then decide to *live* in the bitterness of betrayal, and begin to manipulate other people, I lose the possibility of enjoying me. I remain on empty. I think that's sad because I don't see anything wrong with wanting to enjoy who we are and who we can become, even if it's doing something like going for a run.

T: And the tragedy is we become so focused on the betrayer that we fail to enjoy those who truly love us. We may even begin to view everyone as potential betrayers. By doing this we cause harm to ourselves and to those we love.

You said the tragedy of betrayal is the loss of connecting with who you really are, and also perceiving others as potential betrayers. How long does it take to get back to authentic living?

Healing Stages

J: Well, if we're getting into betrayal like we've experienced a death then we'll have to go through a grieving process. The clinical answer for dealing with the death of a loved one suggests we'll all go through a numbing stage, which we have to negotiate because that's where life goes after the loss.

Generally, it can be two to three months before people begin to transition out of the numbing stage, which starts by entering into and feeling more of the loss.

Typically, by the sixth month they'll make a transition to reorganize their life. But I say typically because some may take longer, and that's okay. If we're talking about going back into society, where a person gets their grieving work done, it might even take a couple of years.

But, something is different about experiencing a death from betrayal when it comes from a close personal friend, a husband, a spouse, or a child who betrayed his or her parents. When that happens we will have to go through a process of feeling it in a similar yet dissimilar way, because the betrayer is still alive.

We may have to navigate contact with them as we learn what it means to live with the bitterness instead of being in the bitterness of betrayal. We may even get to the point where we viscerally feel the betrayal and emotionally absorb it. This is not going to be out of sight, out of mind stuff.

So, the thing about going through this grieving process, whether we like it or not, is how it's going to affect our relationship with the betrayer. We have to do it. There are no choices about that. But what impact will it have? How—and how much—will it affect us?

If I'm hit by a car and manage to survive, I've got to deal with broken limbs. I will be up on the gurney whether I like it or not, but I have to do it. It's the same way in the grieving process. It's not about just *getting over it* as some might want to believe.

It's amazing how people try to play games in their minds when it comes to grieving over relational betrayals. Sometimes they think all they have to do is *get busier* as you mentioned you did, instead of doing the grieving work. But when they're betrayed it's a death! So they're hit with some bitterness they must experience if they want to get healthy.

By the way, I don't believe it's wrong to experience bitterness, but I think it's really dangerous and destructive to *be* bitter, which is a different thing.

Being bitter, rather than experiencing bitterness, is a choice people make to protect themselves like the turtle, only this bitter shell becomes an attitude they put on to make sure they're not vulnerable again. Ever!

There is a real possibility that people fail to heal because they don't or won't go through the pain and bitterness that's required. When the victim of betrayal makes that choice they can lose their sense of authenticity and stop having meaningful relationships.

T: What determines the time it will take to work through being betrayed?

J: I think it depends on the level of betrayal. It depends on who betrays us. In my life, there have been people who hurt me that weren't close to me, so their betrayal seemed to be no more than a mosquito bite.

But other people had power in my life, not like the power of an employer over an employee but more like the power I gave to them to speak into my life. And then, their betrayal felt like I was being ripped by an alligator!

There's no way around having to go through the bitterness of something like that. We'll have to feel the pain and experience being angry. The wound is deep, and Elizabeth Kubler-Ross's stages of grieving won't matter if they're viewed only as academic, sequential steps to go through.[3]

So it's really particular to each individual. As we've already established it still takes somewhere between six months to a year to be able to operate without the betrayal determining whether we function *well* or not. Of course there will be exceptions, but once a given betrayal has been identified and we start to reorganize our life, the memory of that betrayal can still linger.

We might have become productive or arrived at the place where we're a little more vulnerable with people who haven't betrayed us in the past. But there are times when the name of the betrayer comes up again. In that moment, time and space become irrelevant.

Like it or not, we'll have to emotionally renegotiate the betrayal as if it just happened. The difference is that this part of the grieving process can last only minutes instead of months or years. When that happens, we're moving toward health. We've probably worked on boundary setting in our relationships.

In my experience I find that people aren't educated about these issues as much as I once supposed. They often think, "I've gone through the grieving process. I'll get over it and get on down the road." Well, it doesn't happen that way just because we decide to be proactive.

Yes, we can get to a point where the betrayal doesn't affect us in the way it did before; to a place where it may feel like a mosquito bite. How? By reorganizing our lives and trading the betrayer in for new relationships. But the tragedy of betrayal includes the damage it does to our psyche; our soul. I don't think there's an easy answer here. For each individual the recovery time will be different.

T: And you damage the people around you because you pass your grief and bitterness on to those you love. You become so involved with your betrayer during the process of dealing with your own grief that you don't give your time and emotions to the ones who love you. Is that a fair statement?

J: Yes, that's the tight spot we're in.

On some level, we're stuck with this dilemma as a part of the process as well. But if we're going to lean toward being healthy we've got to feel or embrace the pain. There's no other way around it even if we wish there was. Honestly, there have been times when I've wanted to escape the pain too.

I certainly don't think we have to go out and choose to get betrayed so we can feel pain and get on with life. I don't want you to hear that because it would be masochistic!

Again, when we've been betrayed we've got to feel the pain, the loss, the damage, and then renegotiate how we're going to work out trusting other people again. If we don't or won't do that, *relational rigor mortis* sets into our being and we become stiff, hard and lifeless like that Heisman Trophy you mentioned.

Therefore, we must make the decision to be alive and love well if we're going to restore ourselves.

This brings up another tragedy of betrayal. It happens when the victim of betrayal is at that crossroad and chooses to be relationally dead—a very, very sad thing.

Welcome to the Table Talk: How long do you thing it takes for a hurt to turn into a scab and eventually into a scar? What events or words can break open a scab and start the bleeding again?

2

RELATIONAL ZOMBIES

There are people who've died physically because of alcohol abuse and other vices. Others have died emotionally to negotiate being physically alive. Either way they usually leave others in a wake of destruction.

Relational zombies go to certain places just to feel something physically, or to stop thinking about anything that's unsatisfying or unexciting. These people actually refuse to be soulfully alive, and some will do this to medicate themselves through the pain of betrayal.

Come into a room where a young lady speaks about the distance in her family. See the longing to have a father who is tender toward her rather than calling for perfection in everything she does.

Listen to her weep about a mother more interested in keeping up appearances instead of having an open and honest relationship with her. Academically and socially, the pressure to perform is always on.

Then she discloses that she has become a *cutter*. Quietly and secretly, the young lady has found a way to deal with the *emotional* pain of being alone in her family, by causing her own physical pain. Strangely, the pain she causes herself makes her feel better even though she'll leave scars. Why? Because that is pain she can control, and the endorphins trigger a false sense of life.

IF ONLY

Afterwards she turns into a relational zombie, numb to her actual aloneness within her family. The sense of abandonment disappears for another day as she hides who she is to fit into her zombie family.

If only her dad could be strong and involved. If only her mother could be receptive to being real. But alas, the betrayal of parents who say they love her and don't is too hard to bear. Tomorrow brings another opportunity to *cut* and *hide* again.

Betrayal puts us through pain we don't want. We could think, "Damn the betrayer who did this!" But somewhere through it all, if we're committed to struggling we can come to the place at which we can move beyond it.

The timing of how quickly we heal may have much to do with where we believe our authority for living really lies. If that's a healthy concept, when we come out on the other side of betrayal we can be willing to take another risk and at that point, we can become relationally alive.

We can give ourselves up for the sake of somebody else. We're stepping back on the track to loving better by not allowing the betrayer more power than what they had at the moment of betrayal. Then the tragedy of being betrayed is no longer the focus of our lives.

FOOLING OURSELVES

T: This brings up another tragedy of betrayal. We can be so self-focused that we think it's all about the other person.

In reality we are all betrayers at some point. We tend to make the other person the focus of betrayal and deny that we're betraying others with our own actions. We *fool* ourselves and that's the tragedy.

This can start when we begin feeling vulnerable and then put up walls to shut others out. But in reality we are betraying the relationship.

J: Tom, this is true. Throughout my career I've worked with people who immediately take the *victim* stance or get into martyr thinking. They act as if they're betrayed when they haven't been, just because someone blocked their goals.

Many people are genuine victims of betrayal, but it's still possible for them to live like victims by playing the role of the martyr.

As a result they're on their way to becoming victimizers themselves, because they've got to learn how to twist relationships so they can remain in control. The thinking goes like this: "I am *NOT* going to have anyone hurt or damage me like that again!"

However, if they think that having that attitude doesn't become a springboard for becoming the betrayer they never thought they could be, they're fooling themselves.

Welcome to the Table Talk: Think of a time when you felt like a victim or played the victim when you weren't. Would you consider writing out what part you played in the action or event?

A Dark Side

T: Let's flip that coin over. What about the person who enjoys being the betrayer? That's also a tragedy, isn't it? This individual is bent on taking advantage of others. Maybe a good illustration comes from the game of checkers where the idea is, I jump you; you crown me.

J: To start with, I don't believe anyone is born a betrayer because the act of betrayal *has* to be a choice. So individuals who get their excitement by jerking other people's chains to destroy, extort, con, or rob them of their identity weren't created to do so. **It was a choice**.

When a thief goes on line with your credit card to hack your accounts and ruin your life, they have deliberately chosen to go to the dark side. There are terms in the counseling community to describe individuals who choose to live like that, such as *sociopath* or *psychopath*.

Those labels describe emotionally vacant people who have no sense of empathy toward others. They've lost their sense of humanity and cannot walk a mile in your moccasins. For them, if they can hurt you, it's exhilarating!

These people believe being and doing evil is okay. Life is one big virtual reality game, and they make the rules. They decide to hurt you just because they can.

We have a world full of people like this.

T: Jerry, you and I have talked about how this can even be within churches. People can appear squeaky clean and use all the right words. They may even be well-known leaders. Then suddenly they are in the news for illegal or immoral behavior.

Too often people like this, rather than being broken by their behavior, just move on to other organizations. They don't care if others are hurt because it is all about them. The lord of their lives is self; they only care about how *they* look. Life is about manipulation and seeing other people as objects to possess. This is evil!

Doesn't that play right in to arrogant thinking?

Entitled

J: Yes! They might not literally stand in front of a mirror and say, "I am different and better than anybody else," but that's the way they live out their lives.

People who buy into this arrogance believe they are entitled, and that everybody should understand them so they can catch a break. This type of betrayer will raise havoc with their family and their community. They'll repeat all kinds of negative behaviors to confirm their belief about this cornerstone of their self-image.

Tom, as we've been talking about the real tragedy of being betrayed or of being the betrayer, there has been something on my mind. No doubt people can tell us stories to demonstrate this, but I'm curious about where you think betrayal begins.

T: Well, I think betrayal starts in the mind. When two people have different agendas, the betrayer chooses to do his own thing rather than honestly talking through the issue. The betrayer may inwardly be angry or believe they're better.

J: As you say that you remind me of my work with habitually irresponsible, twisted thinkers who've been in trouble with the law or with other relationships. I can say without exception that just the thought of betraying somebody is exciting to them.

T: It's a thrill!?

J: Sure! In their minds it's, "Can I betray this guy without him knowing it?" Or, "Can I do it 'just right' because I want others to know when I'm done that they can't do anything about it?" The thought of betrayal is always, "Can I get the advantage?"

I mean, we are talking about individuals who mess with people just for the heck of it. In their view, if people are too dumb to figure it out, that's their bad.

> **Welcome to the Table Talk:** Do you have talents or gifts that might make you think you're different and better than someone else? What safeguards can you install to keep from acting on these thoughts?

THE ANGER FANTASY

T: So, is it aggressive or passive-aggressive anger, or is it a little of both?

J: I agree that it starts in the mind, but in a different way. Even though this anger eventually comes off as aggressive or passive-aggressive, the seed for unleashing this energy starts to germinate when a person begins thinking they are *superior* to others. Nobody is going to disturb that image and they *will* betray you to guarantee that it remains intact. This mental picture is central to why they betray people, but it's a fantasy they keep secret until it becomes public.

Guys in trouble with pornography will do that. The excitement of pursuing pornography is obviously a secret. They don't go to their wives and say, "Okay, Suzy Q, this is something I really like doing and I hope you like it too. Will you give me permission to indulge in it?"

I know I'm being absurd by thinking men would actually do that. But fundamentally, it's important to know that *within the secret* lies the idea of being superior to their spouse. I've seen it often in the counseling arena.

T: Some people have no moral concerns with pornography. They may even bring their partner into the fantasy and say, "Come on, let's watch this together and then get it on. We may even learn some stuff." Is this betrayal?

J: Yes. There's an irresponsible fantasy going on somewhere in their minds. All of us fantasize. It's impossible not to. The issue is whether our fantasies are going to be responsible or irresponsible.

In the case you've mentioned, the guy has an irresponsible fantasy that his wife most likely doesn't know about. And, like I stated, it's used to substantiate his idea that he's superior to her—or anyone else, for that matter.

If we're tracking the way this guy thinks, he'll immediately satisfy himself when he's bored. *Boredom* says he's not as unique as he thinks he is.

And so the betrayal originates in how a person can seem to be someone else, but if others really knew that person's fantasy life they would absolutely be betrayed. Tom, that's the agenda thing you talked about and it's an angry agenda that demands fantasy for satisfaction.

Welcome to the Table Talk: Is there such a thing as righteous anger? If so, who determines what is righteous? How much flesh must someone take to have his anger leave? Has anything ever happened to you when, out of anger, you went over the edge to become a first degree, pro-active betrayer?

BETRAYER AGENDAS

T: Don't we all have agendas? Or are you talking about an agenda that is intentionally harmful?

J: Yes to both questions, Tom. Let me illustrate.

What if I were to fantasize about beating somebody up to satisfy a thirst for revenge? Because a person ticked me off, this thirst becomes a fantasy I plug into anytime I want. I make a decision not to say I think he's a jerk, but in my mind I'm beating the tar out of him.

I maintain that secret in my own personal virtual reality and no one else is going to know about it. Why? In my own mind I'm in absolute and complete control of him and anything else.

Hey, I've been with preachers on a golf course who named a golf ball after a certain elder or deacon, so they could slam the ball down the fairway and laugh about it afterwards! They know they're making that decision. It's not like, "Oops! What did I do? I didn't know that!"

There is a definite point in time when people hone into their decision making even if it takes only a micro-second. They know and have decided they're not going to tell the truth. They'll think "I am going to tell half-truths because it benefits me."

So, this is more than thinking somebody is a jerk and then wondering if I should tell them. That wouldn't be a fantasy thing to me, but it might be the polite thing to do.

Yet if anyone, with forethought, creates a fantasy to hurt or control another individual, *it becomes and is the agenda*. Sadly, that fantasy eventually finds its way out into the real world, and we can all point to instances where this has happened.

T: I remember that as a child I imagined myself batting like Hank Aaron or Joe Adcock, or pitching like Juan Marichal, Lou Burdette, or Warren Spahn. I wanted to be just like them!

So you're saying in a similar way, the betrayer has in his mind an image of who he is. He has this baseball card of himself in his mind. He has his own style and relishes it and he hopes that people notice.

So it seems fair to say that there are different kinds of betrayal styles.

3

BETRAYER STYLES

To have style usually suggests a flair for flamboyance, finesse, and feel. We see it in all walks of life—the sports world, fashion, theater, music, politics, religion, medicine, writing, and the culinary field to name just a few.

Style can depict core desires for expressing individuality and uncommonness. Good taste and discernment are noteworthy characteristics in the pursuit of excellence, upholding the brand we offer to make the world a better place. That is style at its best.

But style can denote something far more sinister when we look at its polar opposites. Related to pretentiousness, which is a posing of self-importance and narcissism that suffocates relationships, style can mean the method or technique used to make the world ours and nobody else's.

It's a mindset of entitlement; to get in the way of someone else's style is to face a betrayer head on for no other reason than being in their way. It can be about personality, but more often than not it's about choices anyone could make to ensure certainty or control over other people.

Betrayer styles don't reflect people at their best but at their worst. We must investigate what such people look like and what they do to bring turmoil and disorder to so many. On the one hand the goal of this discussion is to warn you, and on the other hand it's to discourage the bent we all have.

The Dimwit

J: Tom to answer your observation about betrayers having certain images of themselves, or their *modus operandi*, the first style I see is called the *Dimwit*.

T: How do you spell that? d—I—m—w—I—it?

J: Funny, but no. It's with a capital "D" although I like the way you capitalized the "I."

The Dimwit is a betrayer, but they'll tell you they didn't really mean to do it and most likely they didn't. It's like a proverbial slip of the tongue in which a person releases some confidential information and then says, "Uh-oh, I'm sorry. I didn't mean to say that." But in their dimwittedness they've betrayed another party.

T: That sounds like the kind of person who doesn't like dead air. As a result they talk too much and often share information they shouldn't. Their intent isn't to hurt others but the impact is betrayal. Right, Jerry?

J: Yes. And it's interesting how they intentionally emphasize what they've done as unintentional.

Instead of saying "I was wrong in what I said and I betrayed your confidence," they don't or won't call it out. They'd rather plead for understanding and suggest they didn't mean to destroy your life. That's so you can see they're still a good person. After that, the victim is supposed to forget about it.

Their demand to be liked can be insatiable! I wish I was making this stuff up but I'm not. This is how dimwitted betrayers affect other people.

T: How do you handle this type of person who is so fluid with his mouth? Do you become less vulnerable and more guarded with them? Do you change your relational style once you know their style?

J: Well, I'd want to know if the man or woman accepts responsibility for it. If they pursue the "I didn't intend to mess up line" and pull on me to minimize the betrayal, I will treat them like a Dimwit. In other words, I won't share information with them because they are toxic! It's a big red flag.

The idea is one of not casting pearls before swine. If you do, they may trample them under their feet and then turn on you to tear you to pieces. They can't be trusted because they don't accept responsibility for their verbal fluidity, no matter how much they beg for understanding.

Tom, being naive about the trustworthiness of a Dimwit's willful naivety is harmful. People lay in the wake of their betrayals because Dimwits won't own that naïveté. You'll rarely ever hear them ask you to forgive them, and many folks have suffered the consequences as a result.

T: They have diarrhea of the mouth.

J: True. Now, if they'd say, "I didn't intend to do that and what I did was wrong; will you forgive me?" and if they understand the pain they've caused, then most likely they'll be more sincere in wanting to correct it. If they ask me to forgive them I'm thinking, "Hey, we can work with that!" By the way, I'm also very glad to have been a forgiven dimwitted betrayer myself. I mean . . . it happens!

Instead of trying to explain how they didn't intend to do what they did, change for a dimwitted betrayer is to focus on the impact of their betrayal and be broken by it.

T: So the Dimwit doesn't necessarily have an agenda; it's just that the person's brain isn't engaged.

Some believe that if you always tell the truth you won't have to worry about what you say. This is not true, because when you have been given a truth you are not always free to share that truth. It might betray a confidence. We need to filter our words!

J: I agree with that. I think most us have been dimwitted betrayers, or will be at some point in our lives. Scary thought, but true. Most, if not all, have said something that was inappropriate or have inadvertently divulged something confidential.

There have been times in our marriage when Judy and I would be taking a walk and having a lively discussion. And in the argument I have raised my voice concerning something I was displeased about.

On one occasion I said something I should not have said. She was looking around the park where we were walking—scanning the terrain like maybe the whole world had heard what I said.

It was her way of saying that this was a betrayal of our relationship, because I was willing to embarrass her in front of people. I'm not seeing people, nor am I even thinking about that because I'm too busy talking! But I'm a Dimwit at the time even though I wasn't having thoughts to embarrass, abuse, or shame her. Still, I did it so I had to own it.

T: For the Dimwit it's a matter of correction. We have to be aware that words have impact and we need take ownership of them.

J: Really, that's what it is! It's not like, "What can I do about not being a Dimwit?" because the reality is, we all will be or have been one. And, like I mentioned before, it becomes a matter of, "I did that and I'm not going to minimize it. I'm sorry, and will you forgive me?" Then we can move forward.

Now, if it's a betrayal of confidential information we might have to face consequences way beyond the moment. In today's world, inadvertent or not, it's possible to be sued for a dimwitted slip of the tongue.

T: Yes, there may be long term consequences. So we all have the potential to be Dimwits. Jerry, what are some other betrayal styles?

Welcome to the Table Talk: What can we do to keep from becoming a Dimwit? How do we go about asking permission from others to share information we know?

THE SPY

J: Well, the Dimwit doesn't plan on betraying anyone, but the next style that comes to mind would be someone who is much more intentional. This second style is called a *Spy*. Think about espionage where a mole gets in to betray intelligence.

T: Are Spies sent by someone else or are they spying because they enjoy it?

J: That's a good question. Organizations send out people to act as double agents, so to speak. But there are people whose quest for information is selfish even if it's senseless. To the Spy, information is power and eventually they'll deliberately use it to betray you.

T: I think in the business world that's probably why employers write no-compete contracts. They are intended to protect confidential information.

J: Yes, people with this betrayal style *premeditate* their approach to controlling relationships. For instance, imagine the scenario of a man who developed a billing and tracking system peculiar to his company, which was better than that of any other company in the market.

Then his company merges with another corporation and they get his expertise on how to do the billing and keep the clientele in line. So the fellow trains this new corporation on his system.

Afterwards, the merging company repossesses the information and then decides to fire the guy. The man is left with nothing! He's out and may even lose tenure in terms of his retirement. Tom, I've seen this type of scenario repeated in the business world.

T: This can also happen in a church setting. The Spy attends a meeting and asks what appears to be an honest question. But the intent of the question is to use the information in some other way. Their purpose may be to influence a vote, to harm another individual, or promote a personal agenda. They are intentional. Their question sounds genuine but the agenda is that of a Spy.

J: We may think, "Wow, they are interested in me!" But really they're going to take your words to make a sound bite, whether it's a verbal or visual sound bite. And then they'll insert it into a situation in which you are totally vulnerable. And it's not even the truth!

We see this happening with people the media has set up, haven't we? I've seen it in religious communities where a pastor seems to be the man another church would want. He thought his ministry was coming to an end, and so he candidates in the other church.

T: I call that a tryout. The candidate goes to a new church and the people are very nice. They like him and extend an invitation to join their staff. And the candidate thinks, "Hey, this is great!" He returns to his current church and announces his plans to the Board of Elders.

A short time later, the church that extended the invitation has a change of heart. Now the candidate is stuck in the middle. He feels set up!

J: Frankly, I've seen the shoe on the other foot too, where a church thought they had the right guy and they vote for him unanimously. Then they extend a call and get a *Dear John* letter with religious mumbo jumbo calculated to sooth the church he let down. It doesn't matter who does it. It's still experienced like a setup.

> **Welcome to the Table Talk:** Have you ever examined your motives for having to be in the know about everything? Did you ever have a desire to have information just to be in control?

THE SPY IN A MARRIAGE

T: Does this betrayal style ever show up in marriage? What about when there is infidelity?

J: I think Spies come into marriages by not being open and honest about themselves or with others. They enter the relationship with simplicity but are not revealing. I have seen and talked with many who realized, just after the *I do's*, that they were getting someone they hadn't bargained for.

Now, I'm not talking about the idea that we are all changing so give me a break. It's true that as we mature we'll be different people in ten or twenty years. Changes can happen within three to six months after the *I do's*. But over the years I've also heard stories of what happens in some marriages right after the wedding ceremony.

Something changed from the courtship days, and I will hear a spouse say, "I got myself into something I didn't know I was getting into." It's because the other spouse didn't give the full story, and there's a total change of character because that spouse played the part of the Spy.

Before the marriage, this Spy will save up *bullets* of information about their soon-to-be spouse, retrieved from that person's relatives or friends. That information may be gossip but it's treated as gospel by the Spy. He will use that information to rationalize his own infidelity when he becomes bored with the marriage. He plays it both ways if he can.

The Spy won't tell their spouse about the infidelity because they have kids. Or, it could be financially destructive. But they'll be emotionally distant and the marriage is then sabotaged, even though the Spy tries to look good in the public eye. Is that what you were thinking?

T: Yes. Do you think pre-marital counseling can smoke out the Spy?

J: I think it could, but not necessarily in every case, especially if the Spy is committed to keeping secrets as their way of life.

T: Pre-marital counseling often tends to focus on basic life skills. But what if one partner comes into the marriage with something to hide?

J: A college professor once told me that when he gives premarital counseling he tries to scare the couple out of marriage, because marriage is sacred and hard work. It isn't to be toyed with by anyone coming into it with secrets. I think he was spot on.

I have counseled couples where men had pornography or drug issues and never told their fiancées they were *using*. They become respectable in business and the religious community, and then ten years later—Boom! They get caught on the internet or get caught faking prescriptions and the whole story comes out.

T: A marriage is built on trust. Do you advise couples to be totally honest with each other prior to marriage, concerning their past (addictions, debt, sexual partners, etc)? I have had counseling situations in which these things surface several years into a marriage.

Is it an outright betrayal to your partner where the agenda is to withhold potentially harmful information?

J: My father told a story about that. He had his first drink at age nine and became an alcoholic by age eleven. His family was comfortable with crime. They were *career criminals*. To make a long story short, as a young adult trying to rob a club in Indianapolis, he was shot by a merchant policeman and almost lost his life.

Dad was sentenced to one year of hard labor in the shale pits at Pendleton, Indiana. While in prison he made a decision to have God control his life. But you know what? He didn't tell me everything he'd ever done. I knew he'd been an alcoholic, a thief, and had beat people up, but he didn't go into all the details.

Periodically, our family would go down to see the relatives and I got a boatload of reality there. I could see everything right in front of my eyes! There was a lot of stuff he didn't tell me, and in hindsight I'm all right with that. It wasn't necessary, although there were things he had to tell me as an adult man to protect my family.

In marriages, I think it's possible that there may be some things a person doesn't say before getting married. I'm open to the idea that going into every detail isn't always all that productive or necessary.

Yet, I do think it's wise to look and see if other people have been damaged by past behaviors. If this information could get to a future spouse, I recommend telling them first before someone else does.

Obviously, if an STD is part of the equation I think the sexual lifestyle has to be a part of the conversation to build a no secrets policy in the relationship. So much is at stake today, involving diseases that can kill. For the most part, though, I recommend putting all of who we are, and what has been there in the past, on the table.

You know, Judy and I have been married 45 years and we're still committed to having no secrets in our relationship. And that is the whole point—no secrets because secrets kill any marriage.

Welcome to the Table Talk: How can you honor and respect your spouse with words? Who needs to know the details of your spouse's life? Are you sharing information that is betraying them?

THE TRADER

T: So there is the Dimwit and the Spy. I know there's another betrayer you call the *Trader*.

J: Yes. It's not that this person intends to betray you. They want to be friends and have a good time with you. Maybe they even want to exchange Christmas presents. But their mentality is that if someone comes along whom they think is more important, or can provide something you can't, they'll trade you in for a new model.

Maybe it's an upgrade in terms of their career or something like that. Whatever good times they had with you are suddenly put on a shelf, or they simply don't come around anymore. If they do come around they spend a lot less time. They're not even talking to you about being unimportant to them. And yes, the Trader will eventually take on the role of traitor.

T: So, it's a business transaction much like you see in baseball. A player hits twenty home runs and the manager tells him how important he is to the team and his spot is secure. But the next year the team releases this player and gets another they hope will hit thirty home runs.

Then there's the business executive whose been let go at the age of fifty. He is replaced with someone younger who will work for less. Is that what you are saying, Jerry?

J: Yes. They may look at you and say, "I didn't set out to betray you but business is business." Obviously, loyalty isn't high on their list of character traits.

In a marriage situation, think of a guy who's on the internet in a chat room. You know he's in a relationship with a woman he is chatting with but he's not into porn.

His wife figures it out. She says she's hurt and wants him to stop spending all that time talking to the other woman on the internet chat room. And he says okay but secretly continues to do it.

He is a Trader and a traitor. Something better came along that satisfied him emotionally, so he decides to take that and use his wife. She washes the clothes, cooks the meals, and maybe they can have a sexual relationship. But emotionally, he feels better around the other woman on the chat room. His wife gets the message. She's been traded in for another model.

T: There is another style of betrayal. This individual intentionally harms others. They wouldn't be dimwits because they know what they are doing. These are the betrayers I know you call *Slashers*. They almost seem to take pleasure in betraying others.

THE SLASHER

J: Slashers are people with ownership attitudes. They don't look on you as a person who can think and feel, or as someone with a right to choose anything. You are more or less an object they move around to satisfy their own agendas.

I've said this before in my work with twisted thinkers, that any twisted thinker who uses possessive thinking, or has an ownership attitude, practices the embodiment of what evil is all about.

The Dimwit may not realize what they're doing. But the person we are talking about here is cold and dark, even though they present to the public like apple pie and Chevrolet. We see them as the good neighbor; just a regular person.

T: Let's imagine you came to me for counseling. Later, in a conversation with you and Judy I told her what you told me in private about your relationship with her. In my opinion that would make me a Slasher. Is that what we are talking about here? It's not a slip of the tongue but it reveals an ownership attitude in me. I had no right to share private information. It's a betrayal of confidence.

J: Oh, absolutely. In the counseling arena where there is protected confidentially, the only right I have to say anything about something

I've heard, short of someone's confessing to murdering a person, harming a child, or contemplating suicide, comes into play when the client releases me to do so.

But, invariably, there are people who'll go outside of their session and, even though I don't divulge information, will tell their spouse or somebody in their community that this is what Jerry said. So it might be what I said and it might not be what I said, but they are using me as the "counselor" for their agenda.

They might think, "I'm paying the counselor so it doesn't matter. I get to say what I want to say but he can't repeat it." That's called *triangulating* the counseling relationship, and some clients will do that.

T: In this example, the betrayer used you as the counselor to abuse the relationship. They misrepresented what was said to gain the upper hand, and used it against another individual. That's a true betrayal.

We can all think of examples of these four types of betrayal—the Dimwit, the Spy, the Trader, and the Slasher, with the Slasher being the one who is intentionally evil.

J: I think it's good to talk through these betrayal styles, because everyone has been betrayed by at least one type. And if you haven't, just wait! We all live in a fallen world.

Tom, the damage coming out of being betrayed is complex. But as we've discussed earlier, it always points to a tragedy for both the betrayer and the betrayed.

For the betrayer, the tragedy is the loss of their soul life and their humanity. For the betrayed, it's about recovering their dignity and refusing to be dead on the inside. It's about the painful struggle to be authentic in relationships where we can risk loving again.

There is truth in the song that says, "What the world needs now is love, sweet love."

> **Welcome to the Table Talk:** How do you handle a relationship with a known Slasher or Trader/traitor? If you suspect someone of being a Spy, how would you approach the person or situation?

4

THE BETRAYAL MYTH

There is a myth that only certain people become betrayers. The truth is that people in every generation have found ways to gain an edge over other people. Prejudice and discrimination separate races. Governments use profiling to gain control over specific people groups. Narrow-mindedness, preconceptions, and prejudgments have become the ingredients for myth-building. These myths are developed to manage people rather than building genuine relationships.

The quality of a person isn't determined by what we see on the outside. Character is found beneath the surface. The religion or shade of skin makes no difference to the soldier in the foxhole. Yet man still seems to gravitate toward judging a book by its cover. The myth continues.

This discussion is about busting the betrayal myth. It's an honest look at the foolishness we've all inherited from birth. We invite you to join us in this table talk.

Deluded

J: Tom, we've been talking about betrayer styles and the tragedy of being betrayed, but I'd like to revisit our thinking concerning where betrayal begins.

You said before that it begins in the mind. I agreed, but I was talking to another friend and what he said sparked my interest in the question again. He thought betrayal begins at birth. Have you ever heard of that?

T: No, I haven't. I would like to hear your explanation.

J: The first thing that came to mind was a conversation my mother had with my siblings and me after my father died. Not long after his death we were at my sister's house in Michigan, sitting around a table and talking with our spouses. But first I'd like to give a brief historical backdrop leading up to that moment.

When my twin brother and I were born, World War II had ended and, as I mentioned in our last discussion, my dad had re-entered society as an alcoholic and a career criminal. He eventually went to prison for a year.

So you can begin to get a picture of a very young, eighteen-year-old single mom struggling to survive with twin boys. However, after dad returned home from prison, everything was new. No longer would he drink and cost the state of Indiana a lot of money. Those brief details are important to what I'm going to say next.

While the group sat around the table my mother got this weird look on her face, like she was staring into another dimension. Suddenly she made the following statement. "When you boys were born, the doctor told your dad and me that twins are going to be manipulators. He said just keep the twins dry and fed. *I think that's why I never picked you up for six months.*"

T: This was the result of what your doctor said to your mother?!

J: Yes. I was thirty-eight when she told me but it was as if my whole life flashed before me. My first thought was, "It's not my fault!" I was angry with the doctor for setting up twin boys to be rejected by our eighteen-year-old mother while our dad did his time in prison. But there's another reason why the "It's not my fault!" thought was important to me.

As a kid I occasionally felt strange and detached, so my way of getting back into the flow of people was through being an athlete or acting like a clown. Anything to be recognized. To me, I was just a kid trying to be a kid. Yet at times I couldn't put my finger on why I felt *different.*

In an unexpected way, my mother's confession released me. Sure, everyone had this stunned look on their faces. And I think that, out of shame or embarrassment, she left the table. But the fact is, her statement was a gift because it provided more understanding of the *Whats* and *Whys* of who I was and how I could then move forward in life. Can't say it hasn't been a struggle, but it's been a good one.

Still I thought, "Wait a minute!" Imagine being profiled as an infant by this man of medicine! Without even knowing it I was betrayed by a doctor's delusion.

Maybe the guy thought he was helping in some twisted way. I don't know. But the impact of that statement resulted in twin boys not being cuddled, picked up, or enjoyed. The only way I'd be picked up was for changing my diapers?! In today's world we would have been perfect candidates for attachment disorders.

So, it's hard thinking about a baby going from the safety of his mother's womb to a cold world where he is already a victim of betrayal.

T: Some mothers put their children at risk by abusing drugs, alcohol, or other harmful substances during pregnancy. Wouldn't that be a betrayal also?

J: Exactly! I thought, "Man alive! My friend had a pretty good point—maybe betrayal really could begin at birth!" It was somewhat overwhelming as I recalled this event, but it got me thinking about something I'd never really considered before.

> **Welcome to the Table Talk:** If you were betrayed before birth, will you bring the subject up with your parents? How will you go about this? Now that you understand this type of betrayal, how will you change a habit?

COLLATERAL DAMAGE AND RETREATING

T: The betrayal could actually happen right after conception. In fact, it's possible the mother might not even be aware of the pregnancy at that point. It is also possible that she might not care about the baby she was carrying. She might not see herself as a betrayer. So it could be many years before she recognizes the damage she's done—if it ever happens at all. It might even come about when she reads this book!

J: The way it played out for my mother is that she '*bought the farm*' on that one. Because of what a doctor said she chose to behave in a way that would keep her from bonding with my brother and me. That would take years to recover from, and as a child I wouldn't even know I needed to recover from it.

Although mom didn't drink or do drugs I can only imagine what it would be like to tell a child that their brain damage or other disorders came from a mother's irresponsible *using*. I mean for a mother to say, "I used drugs or drank while I was pregnant with you" is incomprehensible. For me, it was incomprehensible for mom to swallow what the doctor said. But it happened.

T: Some people have to retreat when faced with this kind of reality. Retreat can be a sign of betrayal, right? Did your mother retreat from her role as a mother? Many people fear facing tough issues, and so retreat is the easiest choice. It sounds like that is what your mother did when she heard those words.

J: She did. You know, I decided to address it further with her and she's given me permission to put this in the book. But I think what happened in those first six months definitely hurt our relationship.

For her, retreating into those words is similar to how I retreated into being a class clown, hiding behind humor. Living a life of duplicity like that turtle we've already talked about can come out of any scenario.

Some people retreat into their anger, depression, or other issues. When growing up, the truth is that I and my family struggled with all of the above. Unquestionably, I'm responsible for my choices and my relational style. But I think betrayals from childhood, and even before birth, do have an influence on the life journey.

I don't want to get too taken up with the story, so it leads me to thinking about the other side of betrayal. And unless you have some other questions concerning betrayal beginning at birth, I'd like to go there.

T: I do have a few more thoughts. It is a betrayal to act contrary to the way we know we should. For a mother to leave twins laying on a bed and not hold them isn't natural. Your mom was betraying you and your brother, but she was really betraying herself as well. There was so much pain caused by the thoughtless words of one man.

J: I wish it had been different. I don't know why it took thirty-eight years to come out, and why it wasn't revealed until after my father had died. It's strange how things work out, but this information put me on notice. Whatever the past might have been, my responsibility was to move forward. It's like the secret is out and now what? I was freed up as her son and now as a man.

Yes, there's been collateral damage. But the proverbial emotional string had been cut and I couldn't use it as an excuse not to move ahead—not at thirty-eight! I think what happened in my story, and I'm sure in the story of many others, plays into this other side to betrayal that we don't think about.

When observing the betrayal styles already mentioned, there's a tendency to point the finger and say that's them, not me. So, to be fair and balanced, I want to bust any myth that only certain people are betrayers.

Welcome to the Table Talk: Are there any words in your past that you now understand as bad advice? How do you plan to handle the problem?

BUTTONHOLING BETRAYERS

J: Professional counselors have a diagnostic manual provided by the American Psychiatric Association, which gives a quick reference to the criteria for any mental health disorder. It's like their *Bible* for counseling that supplies the information for making a client's diagnoses. There's one section in the manual for personality disorders.

For example, we'll see a category such as an anti-social personality disorder for people bent on breaking the law and harming others. Before the change in his life, my father would have been diagnosed as an anti-social personality.

Another example is a section which offers categories for diagnosing childhood disorders. There are many kinds of mental health diagnoses for children, but in one part we'd see something called an oppositional defiant disorder, and then in another part we'd see a conduct disorder, which is a step underneath the anti-social personality disorder.

The book's information is very important in providing as much of an accurate diagnosis as possible to help in a treatment process.

As essential as all of that is, the manual doesn't mention any category for *betrayal*. Even though a counselor uses the book's criteria to make a treatment decision, a potential problem could develop when considering betrayal issues without recognizing them for what they are, and therefore not realizing what's really under consideration.

Now, this is my opinion and not something that comes out of the manual, but it's the idea of not having a medical model like those that the manual supports, and thereby missing how people are still "built" for relationships. I'm not trying to bring doubt about any diagnosis, but rather to point to another issue called *buttonholing*.

We live in a world which tends to *buttonhole* people when it comes to race and religion, but I think it can happen in assessing mental health situations, too. Movies like *A Beautiful Mind*, starring Russell Crowe, brought this out.

Halfway through the movie we discover that Russell Crowe's character is a paranoid schizophrenic. Yet we also witnessed how he could be productive and make responsible decisions even though he heard voices.

A Beautiful Mind was a marvelous accomplishment because it combined the medical treatment with respect for humanity. Instead of *buttonholing* the character into a category and closing the cabinet door, Hollywood finally got one right.

So here's my thought, Tom. Sometimes I think the idea of diagnosing people who supposedly have mental health issues, and then labeling someone as *that's one of them* could also happen by thinking only certain people are betrayers. I mean, there's a danger of *buttonholing* people even from the betrayal styles we've already talked about!

Granted, some individuals may practice betrayal as a lifestyle, but everyone will struggle with the issue even when it's *not* a lifestyle. As a result, certain questions should be asked if we're going to deal with how everyone will struggle with it.

For instance, when a person betrays themselves or others, how can they step out of character and still seem to be in character at the same time? Is that a personality disorder or is there something else going on?

I'm wondering if you have any thoughts on those questions.

GOING DEEPER

T: I think it goes right along with the arrogant thinking we talked about earlier. The individual believes that they are living a good life, and therefore they take selective ownership of their actions. They see themselves as better than others and manipulate situations to their own advantage.

But I have two more questions for you, Jerry. I'd like to revisit your story about your mom. How do you believe your mother would feel about this betrayal today, and how did you get beyond seeing yourself as a victim?

J: Hmmm, we're not done talking about that yet, huh?

Well, when my mother came out and said something it was evident that she was troubled by the thought. I took it as one of those *alive* moments even though I don't think she or anyone at the table really knew where to go with it. Frankly, it was refreshing to see her grapple with the pain it caused for her and me.

Maybe knowing she was wrestling with the confusion of such an act, and then assuming she could sense the loss of intimacy, was enough to keep me from seeing myself as a victim. I think her owning it in the presence of other family members was huge for me, too.

I wasn't thinking she should formally say, "Jerry, I am sorry I did that. Would you forgive me?" That would be acceptable, but because I saw how the truth suddenly dawned on her, I didn't want to disturb any process for healing that could be ahead of us.

After that moment, we still went through issues in our relationship, but eventually we worked through them. When mom turned 80 years old we went to St. Louis to have a family reunion and throw her a birthday party. It was an amazing moment to see our history and yet know we were okay.

No doubt if she'd stopped to say, "Jerry, I would really like to talk to you about what that did to you as well as what it did to me," I'd start dancing and say, "*Yes!*" But that hasn't happened and I didn't require it. I'm grateful she was open to talking to me when I initiated the conversation and got permission to write about it. For me, that was like a mother who picks the baby up, and it felt good. *There was no more hiding.*

Tom, it took a while to answer your question but I think that's why I don't see myself as a victim, although I can still feel the pain of it. I can also see how it hurt my mom, and what it meant for her to have been betrayed in life too. My grandmother was married and divorced six times, which paints a larger picture of what my mother has had to go through as well.

T: How did you handle this? It wasn't your fault and yet you do not act like a victim, using this as an excuse for bad behavior. How did you get *beyond* your mother's betrayal?

J: During that year it was all put together for me when I attended the counseling program at Grace Seminary in Winona Lake, Indiana. Frankly I had more than enough of my own stuff to deal with. In looking back, I could say I had education, ministry experience, and was grateful to be married to Judy and have a family. I didn't want to pull away from all that by thinking of myself as a victim.

I believe if I had demanded satisfaction I would have gone right along with the arrogant thinking you mentioned earlier. It isn't that I didn't want the satisfaction of having a little talk with that doctor, or wanting more out of my mother, but to demand it seemed wrong to me.

So, I chose to see my mother as a young, eighteen-year-old woman who didn't know any better. For me, the more meaningful betrayal was swallowing the authority of a doctor who said something he shouldn't have. His advice was way, way out-of-bounds! Now, I can say I don't really harbor ill will against him but I can tell I'm getting emotional talking about it. The loss was profound, and it's sad.

My Betrayer Called Out, and Resolution

T: Well, what would we call him? Was he a *Dimwit* or a *Slasher*? What was his form of betrayal? I'm trying to put him in a category.

J: You won't let me drop this, will you? Okay, I'm good with that. In my mind I think he was a dimwitted betrayer.

T: So you can be an educated Dimwit?

J: I'd like to say yes but I don't really think it has anything to do with education.

T: So, educated or not, a Dimwit can be one who engages the tongue whether the mind is engaged or not. But arrogance can also add to the betrayal.

J: Absolutely! You know, whatever the deal was about why he said what he did, it set my twin brother and me up to struggle in negative ways we might never have had to experience.

As I think about it, for the first three years of our lives, Terry and I never really started talking. Imagine that! We didn't know how to talk for three years! Oh, we had our twin language going on, but eventually we'd have to go to a speech therapist to learn how to talk. Of course in those days there was no TV either, so there we were, left alone to build whatever relationship we could.

T: That goes back to this whole idea of intimacy. Was your brother at the table during that whole discussion?

J: No, and I don't have a memory of ever saying anything to him about all this, which is an interesting thought. I don't know why I haven't told him, but I will.

T: He will really love getting this book, won't he?

J: Yes. (*Laughter*) You're right. It will be in this book. (*More laughter*) You know, I think this story is important, but again, it's not that I am trying to say anything against my mother. She knows I love her and that's why she's given me permission to put it in this book.

(**Note from Jerry:** After Tom and I talked I decided to call my brother and see what he thought about all this. Terry agreed that it had a significant impact on the way we grew up. He told me he doesn't hold a grudge and loves mom too. We're sixty-six years old, so I don't want anyone to think this is just a cavalier thing. Arriving at this place hasn't been easy, but it's been worth it.)

J: So Tom, getting back to the idea of betrayal beginning at birth, the reality is that a child doesn't know they're already born into a world full of it. I think my friend was right.

We need to be careful not to buttonhole or profile people as betrayers, but no one will be untouched by it. As a result, our character assessments of people can be confusing at times while we try to figure out who they really are.

In and Out of Character

J: You know, when a kid becomes an adolescent they begin to surmise that the world isn't what it was cracked up to be from what they'd been told. That's when they start testing and trying to figure it out for themselves, instead of buying into what the parents say. On some level every kid will pass through that phase.

T: Yes, we saw that in the sixties. The prevailing thought then was *don't trust anybody over thirty*. I think it comes from these kinds of betrayals. Whether it's the government, a church organization, or an individual, we feel betrayed and respond accordingly.

Don't you think this process happens around the age of eighteen to twenty? Young people want to establish their own identities but they are still dealing with betrayal issues they've encountered along the way? They discover their parents aren't perfect. And there may be other adult role models who have let them down as well.

J: I think that's true. But many times the age is much younger than eighteen to twenty years, which is why the myth that only certain people are betrayers isn't true. For instance, we are all born into a world where significant heroes have let us down, whether it's a family member, a clergy member, or a sports hero.

Do you remember the story that came out of Phoenix in 2008, involving Sheriff Joe Arpaio and Shaquille O Neal, who was playing for the NBA Phoenix Suns?

T: Isn't Sheriff Joe Arpaio the person who puts people in tents instead of jail cells?

J: Yes, he's quite a character with a gallows sense of humor! The Sheriff doesn't take guff from anyone and comes across as his own man—the Lone Ranger. At times his style disturbs a lot of people.

In any case, the story involved Shaquille O'Neal doing a rap song on YouTube about Kobe Bryant. It was a dirty rap but Shaquille said he was just having some fun.

Well, come to find out, when Shaq came to play for the Phoenix Suns, Sheriff Arpaio gave him a badge and made him an honorary deputy sheriff. When the Sheriff heard the rap song he suddenly went public to say he wanted Shaq's badge back.

The interviewer asked why. "Because of what Shaq did on YouTube," Arpaio said. "That was the smell test for being a sheriff." I remember laughing when he said that because it was a plain, simple, and to-the-point comment, mixed with a bit of humor. But the Sheriff was dead serious.

He thought O Neil was going to be a role model, and now he's out on YouTube banging on Kobe Bryant with dirty rap lyrics. So, that was it! To Arpaio, Shaquille O' Neal betrayed what it meant to be an honorary sheriff.

O' Neal didn't set out to do that. He probably wasn't even thinking about being an honorary deputy sheriff at the time he gave the rap. But that didn't matter to the sheriff.

In my mind, I could see inmates looking up to O'Neal and using him as an excuse to disrespect authority. Technically it wouldn't be O'Neal's fault if an inmate chose to do that, but Arpaio didn't want to leave any room for doubt.

This whole incident addresses the myth about only certain people being betrayers. As we've said, some people definitely do set out to betray others. And then, there are those who betray people without intending to. They betray others without any thought of how their actions can hurt people, because those actions simply come out of foolishness. To me, that's why the myth doesn't wash.

We all inherit the foolishness built into humanity, where even at birth betrayal happens. No one can escape being the betrayer or the betrayed. Many wouldn't think Shaq was a betrayer. But Arpaio did!

In much of my work, individuals are often under discipline for irresponsible or destructive behavior. Others would be warned to be careful around them, but they'd say, "Well, that's not the person I know." Have you ever heard that? And yet you know it's true because at one time or another—and often in seemingly small ways—you've experienced it.

Don't you think it's interesting how a person can step out of character and yet seem to be in their character? Isn't it interesting how they represent themselves in different contexts? Who hasn't done this? Why is there such a blind spot on the part of the rest of us, who at that moment are observers who really ought to be *well-informed* observers?

Welcome to the Table Talk: What types of betrayal do you sense happened to you in your teen years? How have you processed them? What about you as a betrayer? When you have betrayed, have you revisited the scene of the crime and tried to clean up the mess?

5

BETRAYAL BLINDNESS

Have you ever experienced the proverbial blind spot when driving? It usually happens when we're crossing over to another lane after we've looked in the side view mirror. We see nothing, only to find another car or truck using their horn to warn us, or stepping on the brake to avoid a crash.

We're left breathless and thankful to be alive! And we wonder how it could have happened because we were sure of our decision to cross over.

Ideally, we are reminded of how big the blind spot can be, and we resolve to look twice before ever crossing over to another lane again. But that's *not* how betrayal blindness works.

In this discussion we want to talk about why it's not just a common, ordinary blind spot that can plague any relationship. It's much more than that and we find it everywhere.

At times, life seems to be full of people jumping in and out of character as if we're watching a great betrayal escape artist. It doesn't matter if we're talking Wall Street or Main Street; the questions still hang in the air. Why is there such a blind spot? Where does this come from?

SEARCHING FOR BLIND SPOTS

T: Well, Jerry, betrayal blindness sounds like the *Big E* you talked about in your book *Transforming Twisted Thinking*. You define the *Big E* as an unrestrained pursuit of forbidden excitement.

I'm wondering how education plays into this process. How many people hide their betrayal behind their educational degrees? Having letters behind their name gives some people a sense of having "one up" on others. What do you think?

J: I think that can happen and I also think it's reinforced by our educational institutions, although I don't think that's their intended agenda.

For instance, years ago I attended a graduation ceremony of a university that costs big bucks to attend! The keynote speaker, a former graduate from the same university, spoke to about 500 students in the Masters in Business program, with several thousand people in the arena listening.

Standing at the podium she said, "Frankly, I think you have accomplished something exceptional, but you need to know that ten years from now you'll probably not be doing anything related to your degree." I haven't forgotten that moment.

You could see students looking at each other as if they were thinking, "I spent thousands of dollars to get my degree and you're telling me that ten years from now I probably won't be working in the same area?" That felt like a betrayal!

In other words, most university graduates are trying to buy what the institution says will make life work for them. Then suddenly, someone is saying that most likely it won't! I thought, how come the institution didn't tell that to the students up front? Maybe then, when the students found out, it wouldn't feel like a betrayal because they would have known in advance.

The fact that a student can acquire an elite education from an elite institution doesn't guarantee that the same institution won't use that education to betray that same person, because it does happen. And it doesn't help when the institution *unwittingly* teaches what that keynote teacher taught, but does not do so *out in the open* so the student can *get it* from day one.

T: Right, Jerry. I don't expect too many institutions tell new students they likely won't use their degree. It doesn't make for good recruiting! So you're right, in this way the institution betrays the student. Yet in spite of that, the student may then use their education as power over others, which is also betrayal. It makes me think of the caste system in India, where there are distinct divisions in the levels of society. Education may give some people the ability to see themselves at a higher level than others when, in reality, we're all equal before God.

In fact, I believe there are those who use their education, combined with criminal thinking, to betray others. Some can even actively think, "I am not going to be betrayed by anybody. You are not going to get me. I'm going to get you." I don't know, I'm just thinking this through while we are talking about it. My thinking on this all started with what this doctor said to your mom. Education didn't eliminate his ability—and perhaps even his intention—to betray.

J: You're right. In a flawed world, it is impossible to escape it.

Welcome to the Table Talk: Can you identify any habits resulting from hiding behind your education or knowledge that have affected the way you betray or respond to betrayal?

WILLFULLY SIGHTLESS

T: Sometimes we ignore the betrayal. We don't want to acknowledge or deal with it. It's too painful, so we move on as if the betrayal never happened. Yet in reality it's always there and it keeps us from being really alive. I think that's betrayal blindness.

J: I do think we need to wake up; to not be paranoid or self-protected, which is natural for everyone to do, but instead to get out of denial and look at the reality of it.

Look, living in this world means living a hard-knock life! There are a lot of good things in life, but this whole idea of betrayal, as an undercurrent, is something we need to investigate. So I think you are right about betrayal blindness. Someone said that it's the unawareness of not knowing and forgetting the exhibits of betrayal that harm us.

At the Holocaust Museum in Israel, I saw pictures, videos, and other proofs of atrocities against the Jews that the world needs to never forget. Yet there are people who claim to know nothing of these things, saying they never happened. They deny reality, learn to park it somewhere and forget about it. Welcome to betrayal blindness—*a willful living in denial about ourselves and history!*

T: Doesn't this happen in individuals who think they are basically good? They turn a blind eye to the ways they have betrayed others, believing that isn't who they really are. Is it a fair statement to say that's inflated thinking?

J: Yes, that's a fair statement. In my book, Transforming Twisted Thinking, inflated thinking is defined as viewing myself as a good person to avoid responsibility for offenses; failing to acknowledge my own destructive behavior; and building myself up at another's expense. That type of thinking requires turning a blind eye to reality.

Tom, this might be a good place to say that all the twisted thinking patterns mentioned in my book will be included at the end of this discussion. Then, the reader can track with us when we allude to them throughout our table talks.

T: I remember when we first started talking about this topic. You said that when a practicing twisted thinker comes along you must realize that they are there to manipulate or fool you. Most are living lives of closed thinking. So just know that when they come in, at first, they are going to betray themselves. They will portray themselves as something they are not. Don't be naive or blind to that fact. They are manipulators."

But everyone does this, including Tom Roy and Jerry Price. It's not right but it is part of the system we live in. Is it ever a good thing to exhibit this kind of betrayal blindness? I'm thinking of sexual abuse in particular. Is it ever a good thing to look away?

J: Hmmm, I don't know if that's the betrayal blindness we're talking about. The person who is sexually abused usually knows something isn't right, even if they are just a young child. They may not understand it and they may try to white-knuckle their way through it and survive, but they aren't blind to it. Years later it's often addressed, especially when the one abused begins to experience flashbacks. Then, at that time, many begin to deal with it instead of choosing to be blind.

LIVING IN A WORLD OF BETRAYAL BLINDNESS

J: It's a different world with betrayal blindness. This is a play on words, but if I'm blind, I can't see anyway. It's similar to that except that "out of sight" means "out of mind."

Do you remember that movie called *Men In Black*?

T: Yes.

J: There were two different dimensions. Will Smith and Tommy Lee Jones could see the monsters but all the supposedly normal people couldn't. And when Smith and Jones had to deal with the monsters they'd turn on this little flashlight to put the normal people in neutral or move them to another dimension. After defeating the monsters they then flipped this light off so everybody could walk around again like nothing had happened.

I think we live in a world where betrayal blindness acts that way too. The betrayal is going on but, somehow, we've been neutralized from even taking a look at it and not knowing becomes the safe place to be. Because betrayal blindness can be perceived as a safe place, if a person is a victim, a perpetrator, or a witness of somebody else's betrayal they don't have to say anything.

Bogus as it may be, it's easier to check out and try to preserve relationships that individuals don't want to lose, even if they're abusive relationships and betrayal happens on a regular basis.

If betrayal happens within institutions, it's easier to preserve and take care of the institutions that are bigger than life because we think they can provide something we're willing to trade for. It's easier to live in the blindness.

T: So it's more than unawareness. It's proactively choosing to forget what you just saw or experienced.

J: Absolutely. Years ago, I remember when news came out about a lady being assaulted on the streets of New York. The whole immediate neighborhood saw it and did nothing.

When I read these headlines I thought, "What is the World Coming To?" How could a woman be assaulted while people did absolutely nothing about it? No one even called the police!

Sure, the guy's assault betrayed the lady, but so did the neighborhood. This was societal betrayal. And if we could put ourselves in that woman's position—my goodness—what would that do to our soul?

T: It goes right back to the idea of trying to figure out who you are. We don't want it to get messy so we close our eyes instead of facing the situation and dealing with it.

J: I think there's also an agenda people try to protect. It's like the switch goes off. That's why I wanted to think about this and take a harder look at betrayal blindness. I don't want anybody to be blind to it.

What my mother said to me when I was thirty-eight actually opened my eyes, not only to how I was betrayed but how I've been the betrayer, too. Betrayal blindness hurts us on every front, especially when it comes to loving.

Welcome to the Table Talk: Personalize any proactive blindness you have demonstrated in the past. When will it be the proper time to open your eyes and dig deeper to resolve issues?

WHAT'S LOVE GOT TO DO WITH IT?

T: An author by the name of Freyd wrote an article about betrayal trauma. The theory is that betrayal is the greatest when the victim is dependent on the perpetrator. A victim becomes blind to those upon whom they are emotionally or financially dependent. As a result, the victim of betrayal is not really alive.

John LeCarre wrote, "Love is whatever you can betray or betrayal can only happen if you love."[4] If this is true, then betrayal blindness is a lack of love. When I think about the doctor who told your mother not to hold her twin boys, I don't think that was spoken out of love toward her. And it certainly wasn't love toward you.

He was in a position in which your mother was emotionally in need of him. He was the doctor, the highly esteemed expert, so the doctor betrayal went unnoticed. In our culture we place physicians on pedestals. Thus your mom was emotionally dependent on her doctor. She was in trauma.

J: That's one of the reasons I was angry at what he did, although I didn't have any real hate for him when I heard what she said. I did feel like looking him up and telling him what his thoughtless comment had done to our family. But somehow, feeling bad for mom and for the rest of us in the family, and realizing how we missed out on what "normal" demonstrations of parental love might have done for us, helped me transcend any real thoughts of retribution.

I think there is a point where LaCarre's statement has meaning. And so the pain of loving involves the possibility of betrayal, which is terrifying to us. I believe that's why betrayal blindness appeals. Maybe people can think about it more and start asking themselves, "Is that what's going on with me? Who am I hurting?"

Tom, I don't want be like some dead doctor who said something to a young mother that created harm in a relationship. I also don't want to be a victim someplace where no one wants to help me when I'm being accosted. I don't want to be in an institution that doesn't deal with me truthfully. I want to be a person who knows how to love even though it takes tons of work. The result is worth the effort.

T: Let's imagine that someone reading this book realizes what you just said. They are now dealing with various levels of pain. What direction would you take them toward maturity? How would they go about facing the betrayal? How did you do this in your situation with your mom?

THE NEED TO TALK AND FEEL

J: The first thing that comes to mind is this whole idea about *feeling*. In the counseling world there are three things that determine whether a relationship or a family is dysfunctional. However, I'm not talking about "having problems" because problems in themselves don't make a relationship or family dysfunctional. Let me explain.

One reason a dysfunctional relationship develops is that something happens to keep the people involved from being able to *talk* about stuff. And, when people don't talk that opens the door to hiding and living in duplicity.

When certain things come to the table, no one talks. The subject is taboo. Maybe that rule wasn't plainly laid out for everyone but it becomes the elephant in the room. Sometimes, people are quiet because they aren't sure how another person will handle it. Or, they don't want to be in the middle because that might also go against their own agendas. So it's easier to keep the secret. We just won't talk, and when people within families and marriages don't talk there are going to be betrayals.

Plus, if we don't talk we get to a point where we don't *feel*, because if you feel you're going to say something about it. If you hit your thumb with a hammer and decide you're not going to talk about or deal with it and then act like it doesn't hurt, you're going to be in a lot of trouble. So, when you're hit you're hurt and you feel and talk about it.

But people who are in a dysfunctional relationship (1) don't talk, (2) don't feel, and (3) don't trust. If I never talk and don't feel betrayal or acknowledge betrayal blindness, it means *I can be in control of that little world in my mind.* And that gives me the freedom to not trust anyone else.

Our desire and hope for the reader is to start talking about this pain and begin feeling it. Because, when they begin to feel it they've begun the journey toward being relationally healthy. Even if it basically feels like hell, they are on their way to becoming alive and authentic. And again, that leads to renewed trust.

I want to see that happen for everyone. And the reason I want to see it happen, Tom, is because it happened for you and me. We both know there's life beyond betrayal.

BELONGING AND BETRAYAL

T: I was looking over the quotes you sent me the other day. The very first one by Harold Philby hit me. "To betray, you must first belong."[5] In other words, at one point there is a sense of relationship. Then the betrayal happens. It takes a great deal of courage and vulnerability to be able to say, "Let's dig in here and discuss what happened." Is that a fair statement?

J: Yes, it is. I don't think it's natural as human beings to think we are built to be dependent. For much of our lives we've heard things like be your own man, be independent and make your own decisions.

Sometimes we think there are people we can depend on. But, then there are times we're learning to be dependent in ways that suggest life only works if there are other people we can depend on. That's a false sense of security.

If we're going to bust the myth that only certain people are betrayers, then my belief is that none of us can utterly and completely depend on any other person outside of God Himself.

Oh, I believe we can learn to love and enjoy relationships, because all of us are built with a longing to belong, but to expect to be able to find a relationship in which betrayal on any level doesn't happen simply isn't realistic.

That's because, on some level, we are all betrayers. I think our journey is to find someone we can trust to love us no matter what. That's what belonging really means to me.

T: We need to be in relationships in which we can at least be honest about betrayal; to admit the betrayal and talk about it. Without denying the other person's betrayal we also need to realize we have the potential to do the same thing! It's important to be open when others point out betrayal in us, and to be mature enough to admit it.

I used to play basketball. Back then when you fouled someone and the whistle blew, you had to raise your hand. That was a sign of acknowledging the foul. Raising your hand was taking responsibility. In the same way we need to admit that there are going to be fouls in life, and get into the habit of admitting the foul and empathizing with the pain we've caused others.

So, is our next step to talk about the betrayal with the person we betrayed?

J: Absolutely, when the timing is right, even though I'm aware that sometimes it may never happen. Yet talking about the betrayal, feeling it, and building trust with others must happen if we're going to pursue *life* after betrayal.

Welcome to the Table Talk: Who do you need to talk to today about betrayal? We all need to talk it out with someone.

Twisted Thinking Patterns & Definitions

1. Closed Thinking

a. I am not receptive (tunnel vision—the only way is how I see things)

b. I am not self critical (emotionally vacant—I don't care how I hurt others)

c. I am not disclosing information (deliberately vague—I won't give details)

d. I'm good at pointing out and talking about the faults of others

e. I lie by omission

2. Martyred Thinking

a. I view myself as a victim when I'm held accountable.

b. I blame social conditions, my family, the past, and other people for what I do.

3. Inflated Thinking

a. I view myself only as a good person to avoid responsibility for offenses.

b. I fail to acknowledge my own destructive behavior.

c. I build myself up at the expense of others.

4. Stubborn Thinking

a. I won't make any effort to do things I find boring or disagreeable.

b. When I say "I can't" I'm really saying "I won't."

5. Reckless Thinking

a. I think living in a responsible way is unexciting and unsatisfying.

b. I have no sense of obligation but I'll get you to obligate yourself to me.

c. I'm not interested in being responsible unless I get an immediate payoff.

6. Impatient Thinking

a. I do not use the past as a learning tool when it gets in the way of my plans.

b. I expect others to act immediately when I demand it.

c. I make decisions based on assumptions, not the facts.

7. Fearful Thinking

a. I have irrational fears but refuse to admit them.

b. I have a fundamental fear of injury or death when I'm not in control.

c. I have a profound fear of being put down.

d. When I'm held accountable I feel lousy and experience a "Zero State."

8. Manipulative Thinking

a. I have a compelling need to be in control of others and every situation.

b. I use manipulation and deceit to get into and take control of situations.

c. I refuse to be a dependent person unless I can take advantage of it.

9. Arrogant Thinking

a. I think I'm different and better than others.

b. I expect out of others what I fail to deliver. **(JP)**

c. I'm super-optimistic because it cuts my fear of failure.

d. I will quit at the first sign of what I consider failure.

10. Possessive Thinking

a. I perceive all things and people as objects that belong to me.

b. I have no concept of the "ownership rights" of others.

c. I will use sex for power and control and not intimacy.

6

BETRAYAL TRAUMA

Once there was a TV commercial that promoted beer with the message, "You only have one life. So live it with all the gusto you can!" Was that company trying to convince customers that life is in beer? Or, were they selling the idea that good living requires you to feel good no matter what your troubles might be?

Maybe they were really selling something else, but this company reached into the emptiness of millions of people and made big money selling beer.

Have you ever been asked what your passions in life are? What we say reveals where we think life can best be lived. Food, places, events, hobbies, people, you name it; we all have something (or some things) that brings us a sense of well-being and significance

To have purpose is good, yet even this can be twisted to mean anything that satisfies us on demand, like an animal on the hunt for food. Life could be reduced to only living or surviving, especially after a betrayal trauma. When we get caught in situations like that, before long, we could define ourselves by betrayal and not by who we really are.

Our next table talk explores whether we can have life after betrayal—and what kind of life that should be. It's not about anything superficial, like beer. It's about doing what seems impossible; embracing the unspeakable and moving to a place where we're defined by love. It's not about settling for less but going for more and starting from the inside where the gusto really is.

Real Living

T: Okay, Jerry, talk to me. Is there really life after betrayal? What does that look like? Wouldn't it look different for each person?

J: Yes, it would look different. But I think the concept of *having* a life is different from the idea of only *living* life after betrayal. A betrayed person still breathes the same air even though they've suffered a relational death. And sure, they can do things like eat a meal and get a job, but that doesn't mean it's called *life*.

Sadly, some people believe they can't have life after betrayal, so they end theirs. Others move on but go through the motions, not being honest with themselves or aware of their real feelings. They'll use betrayal experiences to foster self-protection, lacking the integrity to deal with anything that brings discomfort.

So, to say there's life after betrayal is not necessarily the same thing as *living* after betrayal. I mean, dogs are living on this earth but they're pets! The idea of *living* means nothing if just going through the motions is all there is. To me, that's not *LIFE*!

> **Welcome to the Table Talk:** Would you describe yourself as just alive or really living? What needs to happen for you to live your life to its fullest?

T: Does the depth of the betrayal play a part? For example, we all betray ourselves at some level. We set very high goals for ourselves at the beginning of each year yet seldom follow through. We end up betraying ourselves.

J: Sure. We can see that on TV reality shows. There's one program in which everybody involved works to get hundreds of pounds off an obese person. It's great to be called the biggest loser when that happens.

Some participants feel more alive because they've reached into their core identities and don't want to give up on that. But you're right about New Year's resolutions not lasting long. Even so, however insignificant those resolutions may seem to be, I agree that we subtly betray ourselves.

People addicted to drugs can treat promises to stop using as if they're New Year's resolutions. They may say things like, "I'll never let that happen again," "I'm not going to shoot up," "It will be different this time," "I've learned my lesson," and then go back on their word.

But the gap between promising something insignificant, such as not eating donuts this year, compared to something very significant, such as withdrawing from dope, is immaterial. I mean, whenever their commitment is betrayed, something breaks down inside a person that weakens their approach to specific relationships and to life in general.

T: Let's look at another side of this question. Is it possible to become extremely disciplined—setting high goals and keeping them—to avoid dealing with betrayal issues? Are there those who attempt to silence the pain by becoming high achievers?

J: Yes, that's possible. For example, I've counseled women who've been sexually abused as children by a trusted friend or a relative. Most of them, at the initial interview, don't come in looking disheveled. They're impeccably groomed even though deeply troubled. They look like they have life but dress to disguise the death they feel on the inside.

T: It sounds like the outward grooming is an attempt to appear as if everything is fine, but the purpose is to hide the inner turmoil. It's playing a part, like an actor or a geisha girl, but the person knows that the character they portray is not who they really are.

J: Right! And maybe it's because they don't know how to deal with those issues. Or, they're not in a place where it's safe to address the problem. In the case of an abused woman it could be traumatic to begin feeling and trusting men again. In their mind they can't do that, so they take control of other aspects of their lives and appear to be on top of things in other ways.

I understand the longing to find a safe someone, and I'm not criticizing a woman who's been sexually abused for not being in the position to have that longing met. That re-traumatizes them, which is not what I want to do. Yet, by taking on the geisha girl appearance they do split their soul to protect themselves, and in the end it's a betrayal of self.

I know of an older woman who, as a child way back in the nineteen thirties, had a mother beat her with an electric extension cord. Well, what do you think that does to a little girl who grows up to become a woman? Don't you think she's going to make sure that no person out there is ever going to take an extension cord to her again? So how does she behave to keep that from happening?

She begins to manufacture her own realities to survive. Instead of being honest with self and others, she becomes closed in her thinking, at which point the only way to see things is her way. She puts on the mask of a tough lady so you can't see the little girl in her. You can't go there to talk about it and you don't blame her. The post-trauma is just as real. And as sad as that story is, it does happen.

PTSD

T: So the post-trauma of betrayal can cause significant stress. Most people have heard of Post Traumatic Stress Disorder. Is that what this would be?

J: I believe it is. In the past, that diagnosis was attached to individuals who went through incredible violence and killing during the Vietnam

War. After these warriors came home, no one talked to them about making adjustments from war to peace time.

Tom, here's part of that conflict. In wartime, to be a soldier and kill somebody is morally accepted under the rules of engagement. But the naked truth is a soldier must be trained to use anger in killing people.

I'm not criticizing the military because hundreds of thousands of good soldiers have given their lives to protect this country throughout our history. War calls for an on-the-alert mentality, but it's been no secret that soldiers transitioning to civilian life are often faced with tremendous adjustment issues to overcome.

When they come home it's no longer okay to be angry. In a sense they're not rewarded anymore for using anger in the thick of battle, as they did so recently. Yet they're still feeling the trauma of being at war.

They become hyper-vigilant and easily startled. If they think they're in danger, even in the homeland, they'll fight you to the end no matter who it is. They're good guys but suddenly the Rambo in them is unleashed!

Those who've been sexually abused will go through the same conflict, but now the conflict dynamic has been flipped. They were in their own war zone but they couldn't be angry. They aren't trained to be angry for survival, but eventually they'll have to address the anger that's turned inward.

This next scenario is not uncommon and it perfectly illustrates that thought. It's about women in their forties who were abused when they were ten years old or younger. For years they survived by blocking the abuse from their minds.

Let's say they get married when they're twenty. The marriage goes twenty years and suddenly they'll have flashbacks. Boom! Their whole married life changes because finally they have to deal with that traumatic moment, and it's called Post Traumatic Stress Disorder. That's what we're talking about. It's the same as if she's a soldier or not. She has to address the shock of it.

T: Jerry, you've had some of this in your own family. Do you want to share that?

J: Yes, I will because I have the permission to tell the story.

The Unspeakable Happened

Recently, Judy and I had a visit from our daughter and son-in-law, who live in Green Bay, Wisconsin. Jana and Craig do music and have gigs all over the country. They're called *The Hollands*!

Before Jana and the family came out to central Oregon, Judy asked if Jana and I would be open to talking to the Sisters High School health classes about Jana's experience of being sexually assaulted by a neighborhood boy, at age six. We thought that if the students could see there was hope beyond her betrayal, it would be worth it. We went public because Jana was ready and we were ready. She's done a fantastic job of addressing the abuse and no longer sees herself as a victim. She calls herself a survivor.

Jana was molested for six weeks by that neighborhood boy, whom we trusted and allowed into our house. We didn't find out anything was wrong until she was sixteen. Jana was like the perfect girl. She was beautiful and played high school basketball for me when I coached in Ravenna, Michigan. We didn't see any signs of damage or acting out.

She kept the secret, but in hindsight I was also an emotionally distant dad. Welcome to the formula for living in denial. Makes me sick to think about that, and even though I'm not responsible for the abuse I wonder what might have been different if I hadn't been so distant—if I'd been a lot more "tuned in" to my daughter so that I might have suspected something and done something about it a lot sooner.

Ten years later, I was going through a counseling program at Grace Seminary in Winona Lake Indiana when her sexual abuse came out. Our whole family had been wounded by this, and we went through a lot of adjustments over the years to get healthy.

Since then, it's taken all this time to develop a home environment that puts everything out on the table so that secrets have no place within the family. We've talked about it but this was the first time Jana agreed to present her story to other people with *us* in the same room.

By the way, many more high school students in our country are in the same boat that Jana and our family have been. She wanted them to know where the hope is and how they could find a new life after the stress of trying to protect themselves by putting on a false front and resembling the geisha girls. She had been a person who looked like everything was together, but underneath the mask she was absolutely devastated.

Today, she and her husband are the proud parents of our lovely granddaughter and grandson, but even so, there's much more to the story than you might imagine. I want to make the point that this journey of coming together to do a presentation at Sisters High School took *thirty-four years*!

In those classes we talked about what happened to her and our family. We talked about where we failed as parents, and specifically where we missed it in terms of protecting her. Jana talked about what she went through after the abuse, and what she felt throughout life about sex and guys; the whole nine yards. For some in that classroom, the healing was just beginning. For us, it continues.

T: Does Jana's story illustrate the self-betrayal we have been discussing? Did she play the role of the beautiful, athletic, talented daughter for thirty-four years, acting like she had everything together?

J: Yes, but when Jana was twenty-seven and pregnant with our granddaughter, she stopped the *just living* thing. Instead of going through the motions, she embraced life by becoming more real. That means she spent twenty-one years in self-betrayal to further the damage after her abuse.

Today, as the healing continues, Jana is there to talk with people. She loves to work with those who've been hurt, are alternative, and are into different kinds of music. She loves children and wants to give something back, because she is a stronger and healthier person now.

I think one more thing needs to be added about her healing. Jana decided to go back to her understanding of faith in Jesus Christ and having God participate in her life, which was and is huge. Amazing!

For Jana, the writer of Hebrews 4:13-16 says it this way too:

"Nothing in all creation can hide from him. Everything is naked and exposed before his eyes. This is the God to whom we must explain all that we have done. That is why we have a great High Priest who has gone to heaven, Jesus the Son of God. Let us *cling* to him and never stop trusting him. This High Priest of ours understands our weaknesses, for he faced all of the same temptations we do, yet he did not sin. So let us come boldly to the throne of our gracious God. There we will receive *his mercy*, and we will find *grace* to help us when we need it." (NLT, emphasis mine)

Tom, I think she pictures the person who has *life after betrayal*. I know you and I long for anyone reading this discussion to have that, too.

Welcome to the Table Talk: How did it make you feel after reading Jerry's frank discussions about his daughter? What thoughts do you have about it?

Masks & Minimizing

T: Healing does not always happen in the same amount of time for everyone. It takes longer for some of us to face the reality that we have betrayed ourselves. There is also a tendency in many of us to minimize the damage of betrayal. Then to compare our situation to others and say, "Well, my story isn't that bad."

J: When I hear that comment I have a tendency to think that the person's abuse might be a lot worse than they say it is. And so, there they go again, betraying themselves.

And even if it isn't as bad in terms of the severity, their minimization is designed to put them into a different category. Being in that category then allows them to dismiss the personal work they need to do in addressing the damage. They might not be aware of it but that's how the minimization works.

Tom, I know this can be a hard statement to hear, but on some level, those who minimize their betrayal become more plastic in their approach to relationships, and have tendencies to put on all kinds of faces. We talked about the mask on the geisha girl. Well, we can wear the angry mask, the happy mask, the God mask, the wonderful neighbor mask, and the professional mask, but no one is going to get who we really are. It's all a mask!

Even if the betrayal wound is minimized as something less than what happened to our daughter, the issue is not the severity of the abuse because *damage* is *damage*. And if they're not going to be honest about that they are betraying themselves.

Something within ourselves our humanity gets diminished when we're not allowed to say "Here's what the abuse is," or "This is what happened and here's how we're moving through it."

T: You mentioned the God mask. People of all different faiths, if they believe in God, must see God as the betrayer in many of these situations. How do you resolve that?

The Tough Question

J: My bias about God is that he's not a betrayer. He wants to have a relationship with us even when we don't deserve one. He wants to protect us. But we live in a fallen world where sometimes we do think of Him that way. I mean—this could happen even when we think He doesn't answer our prayers the way we believe He should.

So, to keep from struggling with that thought we might say something like, "He allowed it." There are others who, in their anger at God, put the blame on Him to the extent that there's no responsibility anywhere on the part of mankind for the abuse in this world. And given this mindset the slippery slope continues when we let perpetrators off the hook, since the *God allowed it* comment really means He orchestrated the abuse or the offense.

We also happen to live in a world intrigued with perpetrators. The thought that society is responsible for what someone has done to us is always out there. Some will even say, "Perpetrators were betrayed and abused too," as if to imply that those who've betrayed others aren't responsible for their own actions.

These have been among the medical, sociological, and psychological answers for minimizing the actions of a perpetrator. But then, there's one more place to go to avoid taking responsibility for their behavior, and that's the spiritual. It's easy to think that God is responsible for all of it when clearly He's not!

I believe His heart is broken by these kinds of things, and He's saving up the tears of the abused for a day of justice even when there seems to be no justice this side of heaven.

Nevertheless, if we think He's betrayed us I think it would be wrong to try to hide it. I believe that—even though we can be wrong in our view of Him—we still need to tell God, "I think you betrayed me. That's who I am. I'll be honest with you. I'm not going to be afraid to say this to you, God. It doesn't make sense why this has happened to a loved one or to me. I just can't figure it out and I'm angry with you."

Tom, if we think and feel that He is a betrayer, God already knows it! He's not a dummy and I think we would be more respectful if we told him what's on our minds when we begin the dialogue. Otherwise, we could use those thoughts as a means to reject Him so we could do something irresponsible. It's like getting revenge on God when all we're doing is exploiting Him for our own agenda.

T: Those of us who come from a Christian belief system have read of Jesus' famous cry from the cross, "Father, why have you forsaken me?" This is the man-God Jesus seeming to accuse His Father of betrayal. How do we deal with that?

J: In the past I've heard that explained away as a rhetorical question. But, in the raw emotion, it is what it is. It's Jesus saying "Why did you do that, Dad?"

I know we can read from the first page of the Bible to the last page and figure out the answer to that question. But if we put ourselves there on a visceral and emotional level, facing the aloneness and the utter horror of being rejected—even for just that one overwhelming moment—I think it's a fair question. I know Jesus went willingly to the cross, and he intimately participated in His Father's plan for our redemption, but given his own humanity I still think He still had at least one brief moment of doubt or confusion. Or both.

Either way, in his humanness, he wasn't going to sugar coat that question. In my opinion, it's why I think Jesus can be trusted as a real man. On this side of eternity, what He had to do to save humanity was horribly abusive to him.

Yet He didn't try to minimize it or say it wasn't as bad as someone else's abuse. No, he said, "My God, why have you forsaken me?" As a man, I think he can be trusted because he was putting it out there on the table with the heavenly Father. It's no secret that there was a struggle, and I believe He let us see it on purpose to say it's okay for us, too, to ask His father the hard questions.

So, I'd rather not explain His statement away as something theological or rhetorical. I'd rather look at Him as the man He is and say, "Wow, I think he's teaching me about not betraying himself while still committing to the will of his Father, as a person He trusted with or without the answer to that question." What love!

Welcome to the Table Talk: How do you perceive God? Loving? Caring? Distant? Betrayer? What is your point of reference for this belief?

BE HONEST

T: We have talked about a variety of things, from New Year's resolutions to sexual abuse to Jesus asking His heavenly father why He had betrayed Him. As we consider betrayal and self-betrayal, the bottom line in terms of recovery seems to be facing things honestly and working from there.

J: Yes! As painful as that can seem, if we're going to have life we'll have to embrace the pain of our betrayal traumas. If the betrayed person tries to live by ignoring or minimizing the betrayal, it's like what we talked about in chapter two. They'll live like zombies.

T: That's just counting the days until it's over, and that's no way to live.

J: We want quick answers don't we? Some folks reading this can have cynical thoughts like, "Oh great Jerry and Tom—I'm glad I found out about this. You're telling me I have to feel, talk, and trust. You're telling me not to minimize what's happened, whether it was done to me or whether I'm doing it to myself. Why?"

Honestly?

There's no genuine development of self-trust without embracing this personal work. Yet I believe the thought of not losing our own soul is worth it.

7

BROKEN PROMISES

Keeping promises is paramount to being relationally powerful. Ultimately, promises reveal one's devotion to other-centeredness. For instance, manufacturers will guarantee that vehicles are trustworthy even while being driven at unimaginable speeds. When something in the design goes wrong the car is recalled for repairs. Altruistically, we hope the manufacturer's recall is more about keeping the promise that their vehicles are safe to drive than about making money.

A broken promise means a relationship has been dispirited or devastated. Abraham Lincoln said, "We must not promise what we ought not, lest we be called on to perform what we cannot." When promises are broken the ugliness of betrayal is deeply felt, leaving us without a sense of dignity because we're treated as only objects to be possessed.

The movie *Broken Arrow,* starring John Travolta, was about a lost nuclear weapon which could wreak havoc if taken by an enemy. Well, a broken promise that comes from a trusted source or friend is like that missing nuclear weapon that can lead to untold disasters.

You are invited to this table talk as we delve into what is lost when promises are broken. We want to see how healing can happen when we keep our word, no matter the pain.

KEEPING OUR WORD

T: So, Jerry, broken promises can play a large part in betrayal. Promises can be broken in business, in politics, and in our personal relationships. Often betrayal is experienced long before we become adults.

J: Sure, in our conversations we've talked about betrayal starting at birth.

T: Or even in the womb.

J: And sometimes *before* the womb when sex isn't about love or a commitment to marriage. And then there's a pregnancy! So, before the womb the unplanned child has already been betrayed by beginning life as an afterthought. But I'm thinking of any child already born into this world, like my six-year-old grandson.

Joziah wants to be able to trust his papa and nana, as well as his dad and mom. The family is the first community he'll encounter for learning how life works.

Sometimes I like to play games with him. I'll bring out my hand claw and tickle him on the knee cap. He also seems to hear everything, so I'll call him *big* ears. Then he'll banter and call me *small* ears. I'll say, "No, I'm *old* ears." We laugh and like having fun.

In the game playing there are moments where more is at stake between us. When he was four years old, I was in the garage and about ready to leave. I know this is a gallows type of humor, but while Joziah stood by the car I honked the horn. He looked at me and screamed "Stop that!" The boy didn't like being startled. Then I left the garage and went on my errand.

After coming back, I was ready to leave again and my grandson was out in the garage, still upset. Just before I got into the car he said, "Papa, I don't want you to beep the horn. I don't want you to beep the horn ever, forever, ever, never, ever, ever again!" This four-year-old is a pretty smart kid.

Now, I have to promise him something because he's driving the negotiations. I must be honest, so if I say, "Never, ever, forever will I beep the horn with you in the garage like this again," and then do it anyway, he's going to remember that. The message would then be that he can't trust his papa to keep a promise. He'll take it as an attack, and I don't want to cause that. Besides, he isn't kidding anymore.

So, I said, "No, I'm not going to do it never, ever, forever again but I won't beep the horn today." Then I smile as if to say the deal is a good one. He looks at me and pushes to get never, ever, forever again.

I give him my final offer and say, "No, TODAY." I can promise it for today but never, ever, and forever would be a stretch for this twisted papa. I mean, what if I get dementia or something? I'm kidding.

Now, in the car, I begin to pull out of the garage, and as I do, Joziah puts his hands up by his ears, disbelieving me.

Hadn't I promised I wouldn't beep the horn? Already anticipating I wasn't going to keep my word, he does something like that! The boy watched closely as I pulled out of the garage. I left without beeping the horn, and slowly he dropped his hands from his ears.

What do you think would have happened if I had broken my promise? Even though his hands were on his ears, that promise meant a great deal to him. He needed to see that I could and would keep my word. So this thing about breaking promises starts early for all of us, like it did for Joziah.

T: A common theme in Hollywood is broken promises. A parent makes a promise to a child and breaks it because of work. Too often this happens in real life, and the result is like the old song, "The cat's in the cradle and the silver spoon." The child whose parent didn't have time to spend with him grows up and has no time for the parent. The song concludes with "He's grown up just like me."

J: Yes, that's a heartbreaker. Many could say, "I've been there and understand what it feels like."

I know there are times when a parent can't be with their child, as when they have a soldier serving in the military or missionaries serving on a foreign field. But to think a parent would deliberately break a promise to be with their child shows on any level—and at any age—that a broken promise is at the *core* of every betrayal model we can think of.

Welcome to the Table Talk: Have you made promises to others that you have broken or need to revisit or restate?

THE DATING GAMES

T: Let's move on to the teen years and the puppy love stage. This is a time when young people have a great need to be liked. The dating game can include promises like "I will always love you," but sometimes these promises are just lines used to manipulate others.

It's devastating when the young person realizes that they have been deceived and used. This may carry over into adult betrayal because of the pain of broken promises in the dating years.

J: In my younger days, we used to talk about *pearling* our girlfriends. It meant she and Prince charming was an item, and everyone knew it. If the ring we gave her was actually a pearl, then that really made it special. Often it was a high school class ring, or maybe one of those rings with the initial of your first name on it. If the ring was too big, girls used to take tape and wrap it all over the loop to resize it.

Then, they'd walk down a school hallway to advertize their arrangement. Usually, the guy had his hand on the back of the girl's neck or at the waist. And then, somewhere along the line, there'd be a breakup and she wouldn't have the ring anymore. No longer are they walking down the school hallway. Something happened, such as the guy making a phone call to another girl. She finds out and the relationship is over because the promise inherent in "being pearled" was broken.

T: Sometimes couples agree to be exclusive, and when one of them does see someone else they lie to cover that up. When the other partner discovers the truth, the betrayal is devastating.

This can become a potential time bomb if the couple marries. There is a fear of the partner being unfaithful, untruthful, or false in some other way. Have you seen this Jerry?

J: Yes, I have.

Welcome to the Table Talk: Describe your dating life. Was it one of great pain or joy? Is there anyone from the past you need to forgive, call and talk with, or ask forgiveness from? Maybe someone to thank for your dating philosophy?

SEXUALLY UNFAITHFUL

T: Let's talk about the area of sexual betrayal.

It would be very difficult to regain trust after one partner of the couple has been sexually unfaithful. This can be an adulterous relationship or it can happen in a dating relationship. Can a relationship where there has been sexual betrayal be easily mended?

J: No. That's because, ultimately, sexual expressions are indicators of something deeper within the accountability of marriage and/or a supposedly "romantic" relationship. Going outside the marriage, for personal satisfaction, betrays every attempt at developing genuine intimacy. And even if we're talking about the courtship days instead of marriage, keeping promises and being sexually pure is fundamental to developing intimacy. Let me describe how that can be betrayed.

Usually a guy starts to win the girl by becoming friends. Now this is actually a deeper level of intimacy even if he doesn't understand that at first. By becoming friends he sends the message that he'd like to be committed and involved with her. It's the unspoken promise.

They talk, walk, and share life. They have fun and the girl thinks this fellow is real. She buys into him because he's promised his loyalty, with or without words.

On the other hand, one of the reasons many marriages don't last is that the tone of friendship was never really established in the courtship days. So, Tom, friendship is powerful stuff.

After the man establishes the tone of friendship, sexual struggles could begin. What was deep because of their friendship could begin shifting to a shallower place I call the *love ship*. That ship is above the waterline and is supposed to be supported by deeper soul and spiritual foundations undergirding the relationship before the accountability of marriage. And if the couple shifts to the love ship before this is secured, the lie has been activated.

What is the lie? The relational tone, which the man as the rudder of the ship takes responsibility for, is to hook up with the girl because of sex. It moves to a performance-based relationship, defined as a sexual one. Not realizing that the shift from friendship to the love ship was the betrayal, many couples don't get that until years after being married.

Here's a thought, Tom. There's an old rock song that says, "Breaking up is hard to do." When kids have sex before the accountability of marriage, and then break up, they're being conditioned for divorce.

Essentially, the break-up is a divorce, and let me tell you, the pain and revenge involved with that is just as messy as any marital divorce. Is it any wonder why the divorce rate is skyrocketing in America today? The divorce rate for first marriages is 50%, it's 67% for second marriages, and it's 74% for third marriages.

I believe a major culprit in all of this is shifting from friendship to the love ship before the accountability of marriage, and like I stated, it unconsciously conditions the couple for divorce. That's something to think about.

As you can see, it's my bias that healthy and responsible sexual expression must come from within the parameters of marital accountability. But if sex is seen as foundational to a dating relationship, then the resulting friendship—or any spirituality that might also be involved—is only tolerated to support that agenda. Don't be surprised when the relational tone then becomes one of power and control. And if they do get married, the war in the bedroom becomes the *barometer* of the relationship.

Obviously, if either spouse goes outside the accountability of marriage to satisfy himself, it's sexual unfaithfulness. Maybe there's an affair that originates through the use of pornography. Maybe the man or woman secretly starts to masturbate, or one will secretly start to fantasize about romance with someone else. Openness and honesty with each other is immediately gone. The actual core of intimacy, dependent on deeper levels of friendship and spirituality, simply isn't there anymore. Hope for *soul oneness* is lost, and eventually there's a relational volcanic eruption when the secret comes out. The devastation is incredible!

It typically takes tons of hard work to address the unfaithfulness. It's very difficult, and yet I've seen couples restore their marriages. But when that happens it's *always* within the context of an accountability process.

Candidly, it takes somewhere between three and five years to work on restoration. And do you know what they have to work on besides addressing the act of sexual unfaithfulness? They must work on developing deeper levels of friendship and spiritual compatibility that should have been there in the first place. Or, if it was it had been traded in for the love ship and it has to be re-established.

Interesting how all that comes around, isn't it? And Tom, if the couple doesn't or won't do this work, and then ever starts to reengage in sexual activity without that work, I've never seen the marriage last after sexual unfaithfulness.

> **Welcome to the Table Talk:** In hindsight, even though we are responsible for our decisions, if you were sexually active pre-marriage, how do you think the media, your parents or home life played into this?

Good News

T: But the good news is that we've both seen couples that have worked through sexual betrayal and stayed together. Although it isn't easy and may take years, it is possible for the relationship to be restored. It's also possible that when both partners choose to work on the issues that led to the unfaithfulness, the relationship can grow deeper than it was before the betrayal.

J: Yes, that's true. I've talked with many couples in marital crises who've been married for twenty years or more. I often tell them that most couples aren't even married in the *soul* of the matter until they're about twenty years into the marriage. Generally, it's because they married each other with an expectation, a dream or a fantasy. And that was not all bad, but something was not *real world* about it.

Personally, I'd like to see that number reduced from twenty years to the moment the couple say their "I do's."

But they eventually get wrapped up in kids, paying the bills, and making a way. Then disillusionment sets in because the marriage wasn't what they thought it should be. But they white knuckle their way through it and work harder without addressing their disappointment with each other. As the British saying goes, "They try to keep a stiff upper lip."

Then, suddenly, there's nothing!

Meanwhile, the marriage experiences incredible distance and both partners are on empty. There's an affair, or if it's not an affair one spouse becomes irresponsible with finances or finds an addiction to fill up the emptiness. But, strangely, at this point of exposure, they actually have a chance to be married for the first time, because it's all out on the table.

Now—I hope you're not hearing me say, "Go out and have an affair so you can have a chance to be married," because that's the wrong way to go about it! Yes, I have seen unfaithful couples go to that deeper level of intimacy never before dreamed of, but in the meantime there can be an enormous amount of damage and pain.

And, when they get rid of goofy ideas about sex that they brought into the marriage in the first place, they can finally become friends because the love ship isn't the foundation anymore.

In my work with *MORE Married Weekends,* and in doing marital intensives, I've seen close to eighty percent of the couples restored to their marriage. It usually begins to happen when the promise breaker owns up and goes through the hard work of surrendering to and facilitating the accountability process.

Part of that process is to be open and honest on a daily basis. The couple must stop the dance of taking care *of* each other and learn what it means to care *for* each other. When the timing is right they can then address the pain of marital failure.

After struggling through all the above, sex can become an expression of deeper levels of intimacy instead of being the end all expression it was first made out to be.

T: Broken promises can be very painful. But there is hope. On the journey to recovery, what are the different levels of trust? How is deep emotional trust restored between two people?

J: I know we'll discuss this in more detail, but most of all, I think people need to grasp how broken promises are like lost nuclear weapons of mass destruction. It doesn't matter whether the subject is keeping my word with my four-year-old grandson or about being sexually faithful. We all long for that someone who will keep their promises. If we believe people matter, the challenge is to be that person.

Welcome to the Table Talk: What needs to be said or done to get your marriage to be fulfilling?

8

RESTORING TRUST

Ever try stripping furniture down to its original surface? Cracked and discolored wood, sometimes multi-layered with paint and varnish, waiting to be removed and replaced. Time consuming, messy, and calling for patience. Yet the wood's shine—and its original character—can be brought back if we're willing to do the work.

But working on wood is one thing, and it's quite another when restoring relationships where trust has been broken.

Inanimate objects restored to newness are just that, but people have souls in which being connected is everything. There's always external or internal movement in a relationship, and when trust is broken it calls not for a resurrection as well as a restoration. With wood we remove the old surface, but with people we must go deeper to the place where betrayal happened.

As with working with furniture, restoring trust can be a long-drawn-out nasty process requiring staying power. The difference is the lack of a guarantee that life won't return to a broken relationship. Often we settle for any sign of activity, yet long for a full reconnection.

What must happen if restoring a broken trust is possible? Is there ever a time when not trusting someone is to love them? Is it possible to be on a lesser level of trusting others who haven't offended us?

This table talk will deal with major principles for rebuilding trust, to be shouldered by betrayers or surrogate betrayers. The discussion isn't exhaustive but it can stir your thinking to go further. Welcome to the messiness of going deeper in the restoration process, to see if trust can be rebuilt.

THE CONSISTENCY PRINCIPLE

T: Jerry, there's an old saying that time heals all wounds. Is time the only factor involved in restoring trust?

J: I don't think it's automatic because betrayers need quite a bit of time to restore trust. And, if healing happens, those involved might be walking with a limp the rest of their lives, which isn't something people want to hear.

Having said that, receiving scars or walking with a limp isn't all that bad if they're reminders of where we've come from and how we've moved forward.

I've used the following concept to describe how long restoring trust can actually take. When referencing the offender or betrayer, I'll say, "It isn't until they're able to be **consistent without assistance** that anyone can even *begin* to think they've turned a corner."

In the short term, it can be relatively easy for offenders to be consistent, especially if they're in a structured program. Sometimes they can even hang in there with supervision for a year or so. But eventually, what I look for is consistent, responsible behavior without assistance from anyone. It's not about hoop jumping, which happens a lot when someone has been caught in betrayal.

The Empathy Principle

J. One question I have is, "Are there any improvements in the betrayer's empathy levels?" For instance, when a person has an extra-marital affair or deliberately breaks the law, the empathy level toward their spouse, kids, and society in general is at *zero*.

If they had empathy at the point of their offense, most likely they wouldn't offend because there's an understanding of how it could hurt people. But, as we talked about in chapter three, it's possible some betrayers wouldn't care simply because they enjoy evil.

For instance, I once talked to an inmate about his assault and battery charge on a female victim. At one point in the conversation he said, "I can't find no feelings for hurting her in the past and I still wish she was dead." I said, "You can't have "sweet water" and "bitter water" coming out of the same well" and then asked which one he was. He said, "Bitter." I asked, "What happens if they drink out of your well? He said, "I'd poison them."

It may be difficult to understand but this man considered himself a good person.

I think it's essential to understand that for people with zero empathy, their view of themselves is essential to maintaining their attitudes and sustaining their criminal behavior. The inmate I mentioned above actually believed this self-deception to be true. The fact is, if he were to develop an evil opinion of himself he would be faced with the choice of suicide or change. He chose neither and stayed right in the middle, enjoying his evil.

Tom, rebuilding empathy levels is huge in restoring trust. That's why I don't think behavioral changes alone determine whether the betrayer has really changed on the inside. In my book *Transforming Twisted Thinking* I call that an *above the street* change. But the infrastructure of the mind still needs repair.

Welcome to the Table talk: Think back to a time of being betrayed. Have you ever played the role of the one you'd call your offender? What was happening in their lives that might give you a glimmer of empathy for them?

Understanding Trust Levels

T: Trust seems to be built on different levels, just as there are different levels of betrayal. Some types of betrayal are damaging while others are devastating. The goal is perfect trust. What would perfect trust look like?

J: I'd like to push back on the word *perfect,* if I may.

In some cultures, the meaning has more to do with being mature rather than being without fault. So, if someone says they're working to build trust that is faultless, it's impossible.

But a mature or high trust relationship says, "You know what, I'll share with you and give you the benefit of the doubt. I'm not going to jump to conclusions to nail or accuse you. I'll work with you because sometimes people don't understand what they're doing. I will openly share with you because I value who you are, and I want a relationship with you."

Judy and I have been married more than forty-four years (soon to be forty-five), and I would say our trust with each other is mature. But this doesn't mean we don't have times when we sink to lower trust levels. We can go to places out of personal damage or where something, early on in our marriage, devastated us. You know, it's amazing how that could happen. But it does!

I remember one occasion when, after we were married, I was a twenty-year-old college student athlete returning home from basketball practice. In the apartment Judy showed me a new thirty-dollar jacket she had just bought.

"What . . . where? You went out and bought a thirty-dollar jacket?!" I had a problem with that.

Then I became obnoxious and took it to another level by playing the victim. "I can't believe you did this!" Now, I was working too hard to convict her when, in reality, something was wrong on my side of the equation. As I look back I realize that I was acting in an asinine way, because she didn't really break my trust. Since then I've thought about what was going on with me.

In truth I was questioning my own manhood. I didn't know if I had what it took to put bread on the table, and she went out and spent thirty bucks! Now I realize that what she did was nothing in the scope of things, even though I thought it was *big* back then!

We're really talking about me demanding that *perfect* trust be defined as Judy checking in with me for every dime she spent. It wasn't about me being faultless as much as my demanding that *she* be faultless.

In retrospect, that was abusive. Today, I'm happy she can spend fifty dollars, but this is forty-four years later. And during those forty-four years I matured from a *medium*-trust level to a *high*-trust level. Shoot, now we can spend much more money buying a few days groceries!

I now wish that, as a younger man, I'd known more about relationship trust levels. I think gaining insight into identifying my need to mature, rather than looking at the world through tunnel vision, would have helped. And, of course, no one told me then about different trust levels, which is why I think it's good we're talking about them here.

For instance, a *medium-trust relationship* says that certain things others do alert us to some sort of perceived danger, and then we'll put up our guard. We decide to be somewhat open but ready to point the finger and defend ourselves.

Different from a high-trust relationship, a medium-trust relationship says, "I'm uncertain about who you are and what you're doing. So I choose to take the negative side and put you in your place." When we're afraid of something or someone, it's all about self protection. We still say we love a person but won't tolerate uncomfortable situations with them.

In a *low-trust relationship* where a betrayal clearly devastates a person, they cannot, with any confidence, hold on to the hope that their partner is concerned about them or the relationship.

They are likely to confront positive incidents with skepticism to confirm their belief that confidence in their partner is not warranted. They believe at a deep level that the partner does not care. When that happens, restoring relationships to medium or higher trust levels can be extremely difficult.

Welcome to the table talks: If married, what level of trust do you have with your spouse? If dating, how much trust do you have in your partner? Maybe today is the day to discuss levels of trust.

CATEGORIES OR CONDITIONS

T: Is it possible to trust people carefully? In other words, do we need to be guarded, knowing there is the potential of being betrayed again? This is not an enjoyable way to experience a relationship, but under certain circumstances it seems necessary.

The example that comes to mind is the adult who was abused as a child. It seems appropriate to be careful around the individual who betrayed their trust when they were a youngster. Full trust needs to be earned. It seems that even careful trust needs to be carefully given.

We might also talk about conditional trust. Trust can be gradually earned, much like a child earns trust with a parent. When a child is ten he may be trusted to ride his bike to a friend's house, but he can't be trusted to drive a car. As the child matures, gains experience, and proves he can be trusted, his circle of trust expands.

It seems wise to trust in proportion to the level of trust earned.

J: Even though what you say is true, Tom, I think it's possible for victims of betrayal to reject the subject of progressive trust because, in their view, any pain can be viewed as life threatening.

T: I agree it's very difficult to restore trust. The amount of time it takes depends on the damage of the betrayal.

J: Right! As I previously mentioned, beeping the car horn in the eyes of my four-year-old grandson would have been devastating, but I couldn't promise him I would never, ever do it again.

T: Yes, it's wise to be careful about how much you promise. For example, you may see your grandson in the garage but he doesn't see you driving into the garage. You may need to honk the horn for his protection. Even though he'll be startled, you'd rather scare him than hit him.

J: That's true. There are times when offending someone might be experienced as a betrayal when it isn't. That would be a hard call. People organizing interventions to address the reckless behavior of a loved one understand that. Or, sometimes the hard call is made for someone who suffers physically yet pain has to be induced to save a life.

Years ago, my son had an esophageal reflux and needed upper respiratory surgery to correct it. He was only four years old when the surgery at Butterworth Hospital in Grand Rapids, Michigan took place.

After a successful surgery, Judy and I went home but about 2 AM we received a phone call. The caller said, "You're going to have to come to the hospital Mr. Price. Your son's condition is grave." I'm thinking "Oh no!" Numbed by the whole scenario, we realized that Nathan could be at death's door. So we got out of bed and went to the hospital, praying all the way that he would be all right.

Walking into the room we saw a couple nurses and a respiratory therapist cupping Nathan's back, to loosen the phlegm in his chest because he was drowning from it.

His eyes were glassing over from the exhaustion of trying to breathe.

In desperation, I took hold of Nathan's foot and pushed on it. Actually, I was twisting the foot knowing it would cause him some pain, and then this four-year-old boy really got angry with me. My thinking was about keeping Nathan alive until the doctor got there, so let him get angry. For me, his anger was equal to my hope that he'd stay with us.

Shortly afterwards, the doctor entered the room and said, "You'll have to leave because we're going to give him a treatment." I said, "What do you mean?"

He explained that the tubes that were supposed to go through Nathan's nasal passage and down the throat to his lungs were too big. So, the doctor said, "The treatment is to press in on his stitches and create enough pain to open up the narrow passage in his throat." At that point they were going to jam the tubes down, because if they didn't, Nathan would die.

When Judy and I left the room, three nurses were in there to hold this pint-sized four-year-old down while the doctor pressed on his incisions. As Nathan's body coiled, the doctor jammed the tubes down his nasal passage and throat. He got them in!

Today our son is six-foot-four, owns his own business, and has five children. But let me tell you, he was one angry kid during that crisis, probably wondering what the heck his dad and this doctor were doing!

Tom, being a dad who wouldn't create pain for his son was not an option for me. Sure this was a hard call, but in that moment it was about my son's life. So whether it's beeping the horn to save my grandson's life, or twisting my son's foot when it looked like he was dying, it doesn't matter. At first they might interpret it as breaking their trust, but I'd do it anyway.

T: Jerry, we have discussed a few ways to restore trust. When it comes down to it, it's a choice. We start by facing the facts about what happened, being honest about the hurt, and then deciding whether we are willing to be vulnerable and trust again.

J: We do it every day anyway. We trust the car on the other side of the road to stay on its side of the middle line. We get into airplanes and trust pilots to know what they're doing, because we can't fly planes ourselves. Our kids trust that the meals at their school will be good meals. We put ourselves in positions everyday where we have to trust someone.

So when we think about the kind of pain that comes out of broken promises, it's still a choice to trust and accept that we can't control the outcome.

THE VULNERABILITY OF LOVING AND NOT TRUSTING

T: The choice is whether we want to live life fully or refuse to allow anyone close enough to hurt us again. There are many, including me, who choose to feel sorry for ourselves at times. We play the part of the martyr, seeing ourselves as a victim. But a "poor me" attitude is an irresponsible reaction and leads to irresponsible behavior. It really gets down to rational trust. Would you agree with that?

J: I do, but sometimes I think the decision is as much about loving someone as it is about trusting them. I mean, sometimes to love somebody is not to trust them! Think of people who are habitually irresponsible or have addictive behaviors. Ever hear these comments? "I'll never take another drink, sweetheart. You can count on that." "I'm not the guy I was yesterday." Or, "That was then, this is now. Give me a break!"

I think some of our responses to those comments could be, "Wait a minute! I love you but I don't trust you, or I don't believe that but I still love you." Or, "I'm not going to act like I trust you when I don't. You have a long way to go, sweetheart, and I'm going to tell you I don't trust you to let you know I love you."

Tom, it takes a love for the dignity of others to be up-front and on the table without condemning them. But I believe it's possible to love someone and not trust them. Trust is earned. Love is unconditionally given.

This is seen in parenting, too. What about parents whose kids lie to them, or make decisions that keep dad and mom out of the picture and create deep relational pain? What about kids who shoplift and then the parents find out? Or, they're at a place where they're not supposed to be after they told their parents they were going somewhere else?

There used to be commercials on television in which the question was asked "Do you know where your child is tonight?" Or, "Is your child in by 11:00?"

But I've heard parents say, "Oh, I'd never tell my kid I don't trust him. They need to know that I trust them." Respectfully, they need to know that sometimes parents don't trust them when they're acting out, and to say so is to *love them well.*

The real cool thing is to be able to both love somebody and trust them. That would be a mature or high-trust relationship instead of a high-risk relationship, and I think it's possible.

But, however we see this Tom, loving a betrayer who wants to restore the relationship will take a great deal of time. In the process we'll have to be honest about not trusting them, even though we may love the person. Not panicking and being patient while holding the betrayer accountable, in my view, is love and respect for them.

> **Welcome to table talks:** How can you express love to someone you do not trust? What action needs to be taken by you to restore the trust of a loved one? Are you brave enough to approach the situation? If not, what is holding you back?

9

OFFENDING LOVE

Are there guarantees that we'll never offend anyone in our lifetime? What about being a peace lover, a peacekeeper, or a conscientious objector who works at being non-offensive but still finds himself offending others with his convictions? As Benjamin Franklin once said of printers, "If all printers were determined not to print anything till they were sure it would offend nobody, there would be very little printed."[7]

Maybe we can say it's possible to work at not offending others, but like major league baseball batting averages, rarely will a player ever hit above four hundred. There's always room for improvement.

If there are no guarantees that we won't offend people, is there any chance that offending others could happen out of love or respect for them? Therein lays the dilemma.

Mark Twain once said, "When people do not respect us we are sharply offended; yet in his private heart no man much respects himself."[8] This conflict is troubling, but isn't it possible to respect ourselves, love people, and still come across as the offending party or even a betrayer?

Our table talk will look at the possibility that an offending love isn't betrayal yet could still be interpreted as one. Nevertheless, offending love will transcend the fear of being seen as the betrayer for the sake of another's well-being. Betrayal destroys. *Offending love* sacrifices and seeks restoration.

The hope, in this dialogue, is for you see more to life than being controlled and defined by the damage of betrayal. And for betrayers, once they own their choices and build empathy for their victims, to see their humanity and relationships restored. Welcome to the cabin!

The Tension

T: As we move into this discussion there is another tension we need to address. It's the tension between actions that betray others and actions that are motivated by a loving desire to move others in a positive direction.

J: Because receiving the love and respect could *feel* like they're being betrayed?

T: Or at least like they're being manipulated.

J: When I told Nathan's story I imagined him thinking I betrayed him. Yet I was expressing my love and concern even though I caused him more pain.

Occasionally, a similar clash happens when I've worked with criminal personalities or men who are habitually irresponsible or have been in affairs.

Sometimes, they'll get to a point in treatment when I facilitate an A Team where significant people can hold them accountable. The program is custom-made for men because I've never had an A Team for women.

Because these men are vulnerable, in the sense that they are likely to lose something important by not going through the treatment, they have to be there. At first, most of them give minimum effort to maintain control, or they find ways of getting out of the program to maintain their control.

During the initial interview, I may look at them and say, "Look, you need to understand that one of the things I'm going to do here is prove I'm a better manipulator than you are." And of course this creates a rise.

Then I say, "But when you manipulated people you hurt and destroyed them and it didn't bother you. You have no empathy levels about what you've done to your parents or your family."

If the man is married I'll add, ". . . and what you've done to your wife, your children and society. But when I manipulate your treatment, my purpose is to move you towards being a man who's responsible; has feelings for people, and understands the pain he causes them with the hope that you can build solid, lasting relationships."

T: So the difference between betrayal and offending love goes back to motivation. But Jerry, even though our intent may be pure, isn't it true that we need to ask permission to speak into someone's life? And I'm not talking about parents, business owners, or others in positions of authority.

It's understood that they have the right to speak truth in order to move someone to the next level. But with other relationships, isn't it a form of betrayal to speak into their lives without permission?

J: That's true. Without their permission the subliminal message sent to most people is that they have no personal dignity or choices. They're going to have to submit and be treated as an object. This kind of betrayal goes against their humanity because it suggests that they can't think or feel.

Tom, we've been built to have choices, to think and feel, so asking for permission to speak into a man's life is the right thing to do. I won't betray his dignity. Even though his back may be up against the wall he'll have a choice to enter the treatment . . . or not. I think this is important because it seems betrayal can naturally ooze out of anyone, including me, when we forget to respect our humanity. That's in no one's best interest.

Welcome to the Table Talk: How does the idea of asking permission hit you? How might it affect the way you share your opinions, beliefs, thoughts and pains?

THE PERCEPTION OF BETRAYAL

T: In this chapter we're talking about betrayal and offended love. I cannot help but think about the Apostle Paul. Usually we think about Judas as the patron saint of betrayal. But what about Paul? He was a betrayer to the Pharisees and Sadducees, wasn't he? Once he understood the love of Christ he turned on them and became a follower of Christ.

J: Tom, I know you've explored Paul's thorn in the flesh, and you've mentioned a way of understanding what it might have been that many of us would not think of when we read about it. I think it's pertinent to your questions. Would you review this?

T: The three times that Paul spoke on his first missionary journey, the Judaizers came behind him and tried to discredit his message. So Paul prayed three times for his "thorn" to be taken away. *What* to be taken away? Was it a physical ailment, or was it the Judaizers and their intentional attempts to discredit his message? I read something about this on the bible.org website.

The Judaizers of Paul's day had also wished to return to the past, and to take the Gentile Galatian saints with them. They painted a glorious picture of life as it had once been under the Old Testament economy Law. While they were willing to concede that faith in Christ was necessary for salvation, by itself it was inadequate. And thus the Law must be added as well (cf. Acts 15:1,5; Gal. 3:1-5).

The gospel (cf. Gal. 1:6-10) that the Judaizers preached led to an attack on the apostleship of Paul, who had first proclaimed Christ crucified to them, resulting in their salvation (cf. 3:1–5).

J: Tom, I'd like to play the role of a Judaizer and work through their perception that they were being betrayed by Paul. In his resume he said that he had been a Pharisee of the Pharisees, but now he's out preaching a message of redemption as a servant of Jesus Christ!

As a Judaizer I might be thinking, "How could this guy do this? We had meetings with him and talked about deep theological things! He was willing to create havoc by going into homes to separate families because we do what we do *for God*!" But now Paul is converted to a whole different understanding of God, and this comes across as a double betrayal.

T: Paul was well-educated. He studied under the teacher Gamaliel. He was well-versed in Jewish law and held a high position among the Jewish religious leaders. They must have thought, "How can he turn his back on us and defect to the other side?" And Judaizers were against him, even though some of them might have been converted!

J: So naturally, wherever he went they were going to "dog" him and disrupt everything he preached about because they thought he'd betrayed them.

I find it interesting how these Judaizers were doing to Paul what he did, as a man named Saul, to others when he felt betrayed by Jesus and this Stephen fellow.

I can imagine Saul thinking, "Who do they think they are? They're common people. They didn't come through the system like I did. They didn't get a student loan for their education like I did. I jumped through the hoops for this and they're here to tear up a way of life that we Pharisees are committed to? Not on my watch!"

He's so disturbed that he was willing to be part of the murder of Stephen. Now, it's like the cliché, "What goes around comes around."

Wherever Paul goes I can see this thorn in the flesh being what you've talked about, Tom. You also mentioned that Paul might be thinking he has to go back and clean up this mess.

T: And he couldn't just call on his cell or send a text. He had to travel by donkey, by boat, or by his own two feet!

J: Yeah, it's a mess. And in some places where he tried to straighten things out he was stoned and left for dead. People were riled up by this man and his new message. You talk about a thorn in the flesh!

Initially, Paul was offended by Jesus Christ, and now these Jews and Judaizers are offended by Paul. But the fact is, Jesus Christ loved him and Paul really loved the Jew and Judaizer. There are places in Scripture where it says he went to the synagogue first, so he had a heart for them or he wouldn't be giving them this message.

Tom, it's not that hard to understand why somebody might be feeling betrayed when, in actuality, they are offended by someone's *love*. But if they view it as betrayal then they're in what I call a *victim stance*, engaging in martyred thinking. Look out if that happens!

T: Because if we're in martyred thinking we're probably going to make an irrational decision. There is a heightened potential to do or say something stupid right after we come out of such circumstances. The reason we make bad decisions is to make our self feel like a good person, and that helps us feel better.

J: Yes. They're absolutely afraid of something and don't want to be controlled by it. Maybe it's an irrational fear they refuse to admit, a fear of feeling putdown, or feeling lousy when they're held accountable. So they get aggressive and become irresponsible. Like I said, "Look out when that happens."

Welcome to the Table Talk: Revisit some of the anger and disappointment in your life. If you sensed you were betrayed, is there any chance you had the wrong perspective on a person's motives?

THIRTY PIECES OF SILVER

T: Let's get to this Judas character. History has treated him as the bad guy who betrayed the One who ultimately loved him. When we talk about ultimate love it comes in the person/Godhead of Jesus Christ. Yet from Judas' perspective he probably felt betrayed himself. His dream was to see his land free from Roman rule, and he was convinced that Jesus was going to lead the Jews to independence. But Jesus did not do what Judas thought he should and would do.

J: I'm not sure we'll ever know the actual words Judas said about this, but I can imagine him saying that Jews are going back to their glory days of the Old Testament and will dominate the Middle East, because he looked on Jesus as more or less a political figure.

Even though Jesus knew this about Judas, he allowed him to be a part of his ministry for three years. Judas saw how Jesus loved people, but he still had this agenda or political thing going on. Eventually, the betrayal style of Judas would be the Trader we talked about in chapter three.

Maybe Judas had ideas based on his interpretation of the Old Testament, to the effect that something like overthrowing the Romans was going to happen. But there were things happening that he wouldn't tolerate when following Jesus.

I think he might have thought, "Look I walked around with Jesus for three years! I gave up a job for him and have sweat equity in this. I was one of the guys who went out there and fed over fifteen thousand people (five thousand men and their families). I was caught in a storm with these guys and bailed water! And Jesus was asleep on a pillow in a boat. Heck, at one point, there's a storm coming and we think we're going under and he's out there walking on the water! It was a scary time. I've been through a lot of stuff with him. Plus, I took care of all the finances."

Tom, I can imagine anyone who becomes a treasurer or controller thinking they own the business. The proverbial church treasurer could fall into that trap. My office manager is Judy and she keeps the books. I'm blessed because, as my wife, she doesn't do that trip with me. Still, if I let my mind go I'm thinking that Judas might be boiling over as the *controller* of the Jesus movement.

I can hear him saying, "Man, I've done all this detail work and kept the statistics. We've been able to pay the bills and Jesus is going to do *what*!?" I can picture Judas passive aggressively thinking about playing him. Still, Jesus kept on loving him.

Then, I can imagine Judas planning, "Well, I'll take it up another notch. I'll be the point person who spins the thought that he's betrayed his own flesh and blood, the Jews. That can't be tolerated, so the best thing for me to do is to betray him and give him some of his own medicine. No one but me really understands what he's just done."

You know the rest of the story. Judas gets thirty pieces of silver for betraying Jesus, but his perspective was wrong. He wasn't being betrayed—*he was being loved!* Jesus was about redemption, but maybe because he wasn't going to drive off the Romans Judas thought, "He loves these Gentile dogs!" and started to play the race card.

T: Which He did.

J: Judas was really furious but Jesus loved everyone on the planet. Yet Judas couldn't tolerate that, and that's partly how I think he justified his betrayal of Jesus. Then, in its own ultimate irony, this resulted in Judas' own death by suicide. Somewhere along the line Judas realized that he had screwed up but still took the irresponsible way out. What a mess!

T: But it did not change the love Christ had for him. Jesus had a love that supposedly offended Judas because Judas had the wrong perspective. He might have seen Jesus' refusal to take political control as a betrayal, and even though he betrayed Jesus as one of His closest friends, Jesus still loved him.

Welcome to the Table Talk: Offending love is often misunderstood. Please take a few minutes to think through your personal mistrust in others—or life situations in which you have given or experienced offended love. Maybe there

needs to be a time of reflection . . . and then a revisiting
with others to openly talk about these issues.

A Life-Changing Choice

J: Christ's love allowed Judas to make his own choice,
heartbreaking as it was. I believe this love went beyond him, to
you and to me and to everyone reading this book. Yet not everyone
who's been betrayed winds up like Judas.

My daughter Jana is an example. It's interesting to see how she
viewed her actual betrayal as different from the way Judas perceived
betrayal.

When she presented her story to the Sisters High School health
class, she said even though she'd gone through all kinds of pain and
had made bad decisions involving a life of promiscuity and anger,
she finally realized something.

She had been allowing the betrayal and abuser to define who she
was to become, let alone who she was at the moment she realized all
this. Jana said there was no life, no joy, no peace, and no possibility
of any genuine relationship in her future if she allowed that. So,
as she put it, "I stopped doing that because *I'd rather be defined by
God's love for me.*"

And not by someone else's pathetic misdeeds.

Those students were awed by this choice, because some of
them were going through their own sexual abuse either by a family
member or by someone else. They were in their own dark holes and
told her after the class that she had given them hope. Only the hope
wasn't in trying to erase the abuse or pain from their lives.

Jana said, "It hurts. It's tragic and it's going to create some
consequences for me, but I don't have to be defined by the betrayal."
That gave the students hope, too.

And there's no better outcome when tragedy strikes.

As I look at Judas' and Jesus' deaths, I think that's what was
going on here. On his twisted side, Judas chose to be defined by
betrayal, or what he perceived to be betrayal. But on the side where
God loved him, when Jesus was actually being betrayed by Judas,
he did not allow himself to be defined by that. He still loved and
moved forward, and that kind of love is life-changing.

To me, the hope for anyone who's been betrayed—or even the
hope for anyone who's been the betrayer—is that, rather than being

offended by God's love—they will begin to embrace it and will allow themselves to be crushed by it.

You know what? We don't deserve it and neither does the one being betrayed because, when we think about it, we've *all* been betrayers. And there we have it!

Our hope is in being defined by God's love. It's a long journey sometimes. We've talked about people being able to address the pain of their betrayal, and about being able to own the reality that they were also betrayers too. Sometimes being open and honest about that takes a long time. Yes, a long time. But I believe we can move through it, when we allow ourselves not to be offended by God's love.

T: So it really gets down to a choice. Are we going to choose to be defined by what has happened to us or are we going to be defined by the love of God? Are we going to be defined as a betrayer or as one who is willing to work through all the hard issues? Are we going to be mature and stop manipulating or being childish by hanging on to our chagrin, our resentment, and our anger?

J: I agree. And the thing we don't like to hear—and I say this because I'm not sure I like to hear it myself—is what Jesus told his disciples and other people. He gave them the following truth: "Look, if you're going to follow me I'm going to give you words of wisdom that none of your adversaries will be able to resist or contradict. You need to know that when I give you this message of redemption there are going to be a lot of people who aren't going to be happy about that."

And he also says something that would have been hard for me to hear at the time. He said, "You will be betrayed even by parents, brothers, relatives, and friends." And, boy the next thing would be hard to hear. ". . . and they will put some of you to death. All men will hate you because of me."

It's very interesting to see how people can be offended by His love to the point at which they're willing to kill Him. In fact, at a later date, here's a statement made in Acts 7: "Was there ever a prophet your fathers did not persecute and they even killed those who predicted the coming of the Righteous One and now you have betrayed and murdered him." (Acts 7:52)

What betrayal and offended love! That's a hard one. He wanted them to understand. Okay, you can get life. You can have a sense of personal identity and well being. You can be soulfully connected to your Creator. We can get to a new level where we're not defined by betrayal. But I want to tell you something. *You're in a world that doesn't want to actually be defined by my love. My love is going to offend them.*

It wasn't like he said come to me and we're going to be rich, or we're going to have a nice home and everything is going to be okay. He's actually saying that the love we now receive from him is a love that will offend other people. We've got to get ready for this, and if we're defined by betrayal we're not going to be able to do that. But Tom, you and I believe there is life *beyond betrayal* when we're defined by God's love.

That's the choice.

Welcome to the Table Talk: Who or what defines you? Many of us are defined by what we do well; Some by shame and others by education or job. What is keeping you from looking into what Jesus has to offer, and what he really says about you?

EMBRACING LIFE

We have attempted to discuss and be open about various aspects of betrayal. It is real and it hurts when you feel betrayed.

Some of you read about Jana and Christina, and identified with them. Some were shocked at their true life stories. Each is dealing with her pain at varied levels. Jana is now out speaking about how she made it through, while Christina is still trying to put the pieces of her life together. Welcome to struggling through the dark side.

Maybe in reading this book you recognized areas in which you were the betrayer. It's our hope that each of us will become broken and will embrace empathy when we realize that we have inflicted the pain of betrayal.

Nearly all who have read this book so far wanted final answers, but most likely we have simply opened more wounds. You have been exposed to the tragedy of betrayal and are wrestling with some of your own misconceived ideas and myths.

Continue to ask the tough questions and seek help. Seek empathy for others and direction for yourself. Counseling is not a swear word and life is too short to live without direction. If you or your loved one is not open, maybe these table talks will give you the courage to go into a relational discussion that you've never had before. It is time to really live, not just to be alive.

In the writing of this book Jerry and I have become more open to talking about our own issues. And yes, we have many. We also have broken promises too, and we continue the process of restoring trust from others.

As men, we found that there are varied moments of peace and fleeting moments of re-lived sorrow in betrayal. But on the positive side we have discovered that the only long-lasting, true answer to the dilemma of betrayal and hurt is to understand who made us, why He made us, and what might be His purposes in the way life throws us outside of the dreams we anticipated. And we are not talking about religion; we are talking about a daily walk with the Creator.

Seek the Creator of the universe. Seek the Savior of the world. Jesus came to restore the world to himself, to renew our focus on the Father. So, while you're on this planet, give Him the glory. At the same time He passes on to us His comfort, compassion, forgiveness, and direction.

A life committed to Him will not bring instant removal of hurts and mistakes, but it will bring understanding about how we have twisted what was initially intended to be paradise. Jesus is the only true healer of our souls. Should you have any further questions about a personal relationship with Jesus, please be in touch.

Tom Roy
President and Founder of Unlimited Potential Inc
Ministry to Major League Baseball Players
Author of *Released*
A Story of God's Power Released In Pro Baseball

For Information contact:
Jerry Price
www.jerryprice.net
jp@jerryprice.net

Tom Roy
www.upi.org
troy@upi.org

Special Acknowledgement and Appreciation

To Carin Roy

The sense of warmth in her art, for the *Beyond Betrayal* book cover,

welcomes everyone to the cabin for table talks with Jerry and Tom.

To purchase a Carin Roy reproduction of *Welcome To The Cabin*

Contact carinroy4@gmail.com

ENDNOTES

From *Wikipedia*, at:

https://www.google.com/#hl=en&output=search&sclient=psy
ab&q=thwarting+another+out+of+something+that+ought+to
+occur&oq=thwarting+another+out+of+something+that+oug
ht+to+occur&aq=f&aqi=&aql=&gs_l=hp.3...975.975.0.2119
.1.1.0.0.0.0.463.463.41.1.0...0.0.EGxadJmsXac&pbx=1&bav
=on.2,or.r_gc.r_pw.r_qf.,cf.osb&fp=97a3c216a044e6d4&biw
=1200&bih=1470\f

[2] *Close Relationships: Key Readings*, by Harry T. Rice and Karyl
Rusbult (Florence, KY: Psychology Press, 2004)

[3] Elizabeth Kubler Ross On Grief and Grieving: Finding the
Meaning of Grief Through the Five Stages of Loss by Elisabeth
Kubler-Ross and David Kessler

[4] http://thinkexist.com/quotes/like/love_is_whatever
_you_can_still_betray-betrayal/211256/

[5] Quote by Harold Philby: To betray you must first belong.
www.goodreads.com/quotes/show/160419

[6] http://bible.org/seriespage/inferiority-immaturity-
galatians-4:1-11

[7] www.brainyquote.com/quotes/quotes/b/benjaminfr151599.
html

[8] www.brainyquote.com/words/pr/private206804.html

Made in the USA
San Bernardino, CA
14 April 2013